Beginner's G
Google Apps Script
Book 3 – Drive

by

Barrie "Baz" Roberts

Table of Contents

Introduction *5*

    What is Google Apps Script? 5

    Why use Google Apps Script? 5

    DriveApp 7

    Google Apps Script reference 8

Standalone scripts *9*

    Opening the Script Editor from your Drive 9

1 - Creating files and folders in My Drive *12*

    Example 11 – Creating a text file 12

    Authorizing a script 13

    Example 12 – Creating a PDF 18

    Example 13 – Creating a new folder 20

    Example 14 – Creating a PDF which contains HTML 20

    Example 15 – Creating multiple PDF files 21

    Example 16 – Creating multiple folders 24

2 - Creating files & folders in specific folders *26*

    Example 21 – Creating a folder within a folder 26

    Example 22 – Creating a file within a folder 27

    Example 23 – Creating a file in a newly-created folder 28

    Example 24 – Creating a new folder, getting its URL and name, starring it, and creating a new file within it 30

    Example 24b – Chaining methods and variables 32

3 – Making copies of files and creating folders from a URL *35*

    Example 31 – Making a copy of a file 35

Example 32 – Getting a file URL stored in a Sheet, extracting the ID, and making a copy of the file 38

Example 33 – Getting a folder URL stored in a Sheet, extracting the ID, and creating a folder in that folder 43

Example 34 – Alternative way to extract the file ID from a file URL 45

4 – *Moving files and folders and adding shortcuts* 48

Example 41 – Move a file and a folder from one folder to another 48

Example 42 – Move a file from My Drive to a specific folder 50

Example 43 – Remove a folder from a folder 51

Example 44 – Add shortcut in a specific folder to a file or folder 52

5 – *Adding and removing editors to/from files & folders* 56

Example 51 – Adding an editor to a newly-created folder 56

Example 52 – Adding multiple editors and not allowing them to share the folder 57

Example 53 – Removing an editor from a file 60

Example 54 – Giving view access to a folder to a user 61

Example 55 – Giving anyone with link edit access to a folder 62

6 – *Copying a Doc and making a PDF from it* 66

Example 61 – Copying a Doc, creating a PDF from it, moving it to a folder, deleting the copied Google Doc 66

Example 62 – Creating a map 70

7 – *Getting contents of a Drive folder* 73

Example 71 – Logging the name of every folder on the user's Drive 73

Example 72 – Getting the folder names within a specific folder . 75

3

Example 73 – Changing all the folder names in a specific folder .76

Example 74 – Getting a folder by its name, making a copy of a file and adding it in the folder..78

Example 75 – Getting filenames in a folder 80

8 – Getting files by type... 82

Example 81 – Getting any Google Docs in a folder and adding a paragraph in all of them...82

Example 82 – Deleting all the files of a specific type that haven't been updated for over a week..84

9 – Creating download URLs.. 88

Example 91 – Creating a PDF download link and emailing it 88

Example 92 – Getting a file by name, creating a PDF of it and storing it in a specific folder 95

10 – Automatically send a brochure when a form is submitted .. 102

Example 101 – Automatically sending a brochure when a form is submitted 102

11 – Searching files & folders... 114

Example 111 – Searching for files that meet search criteria......114

Example 112 – Searching for files that meet multiple search criteria..116

Example 113 – Searching for folders and listing the result in a Google Doc 117

Appendix 1 - Links to the complete scripts 120

Appendix 2 – Script Editor tools 122

Appendix 3 - JavaScript Basics 127

Further Reading 135

Introduction

This book is part of series of books looking at the different areas of Google Apps Script. It assumes no or little knowledge of either Apps Script or JavaScript, which is what Apps Script is built on. The book is full of examples and every one of them I explain every step of the way, so you fully understand the code and how it's used, to allow you to use it for your own applications.

What is Google Apps Script?

Google Apps Script (GAS) is a scripting language based on JavaScript that sits behind a number of the Google Workspace products, such as Google Drive, Google Forms, and Google Sheets. It is cloud-based and so all your scripts live on Google servers, and not locally on your computer, allowing you access to them the same way you can access the Google Workspace products and services.

The main App services you can use Apps Script with are:

Calendar, Contacts, Data Studio, Document, Drive, Forms, Gmail, Groups, Language, Maps, Sites, Slides, Spreadsheet

Why use Google Apps Script?
There are three main reasons why you would want to use GAS.

1. Automating tasks – It's particularly useful for repetitive tasks, which can save you a lot of time. You can set up a menu where at a click of a button the program does what

you would have had to do manually. It also ensures those tasks are done well. What I mean here is that the program will carry out the same instructions exactly every time, whereas a human might make mistakes or they may do it in their own way.

2. Extending the functionality of the Google Workspace products and services – This allows you to do far more than what's in the current products, making the products more suited to your specific needs. A good example of this, are the add-ons you can download for some of the Google Workspace products, which add extra functionality to the original product.

3. Connecting the products together – The beauty of GAS is that the various products and services can all be connected together, and you're not just confined to using one product at a time. This book is focused on the use with Google Drive, but you will see that it's easy to connect it to the other services, like the Document service or **MailApp**.

DriveApp

In this book, we're going to focus on the Drive service. To quote the Google documentation, "The Drive service allows scripts **to create, find, and modify files and folders in Google Drive**". And that's exactly what we'll be doing in this book. Plus, we'll use other services to be able to do some great things. As you'll realize, usually scripts end up using various services, like the Document service to work with Google Docs and the Maps service to use Google Maps.

The Drive service is a relatively simple one but it's fundamental for working with files and folders on Google Drive. The **DriveApp** class allows you to create, copy, find, and modify files and folders on Drive. Then we can also drill down a level and work with specific files and folders.

Whilst we learn the methods linked to **DriveApp**, files and folders, we'll also be learning how to use JavaScript to do things like looping to create multiple files and folders, how we can create different functions, each one doing a specific task all connected together, and how we can email documents and links for documents stored on Drive.

Before we get into the main chapters, I'll also cover some JavaScript basics and these are in the context of Apps Script, as I've found that most JavaScript examples and tutorials on-line, only talk about its use with web pages.

The examples are clearly numbered with the chapter number and the example number, e.g. chapter one and example one will be example11.

Google Apps Script reference

One place you will use all the time is the Apps Script reference site, which contains all the services, classes and methods, and includes some examples of how to them. Here's the link to the Drive service.

https://developers.google.com/apps-script/reference/drive/

Full pieces of code

Links to all the full pieces of code used in this book can be found at the end of the book in **Appendix 1**. These are stored on GitHub where you'll be able to copy and paste them into your projects.

The best way to learn is to start using it, so let's start with looking at the Script Editor, where you'll be writing your scripts.

Standalone scripts

Before you start coding you'll need a place to write the code. Drive comes with a script editor but unfortunately it's not turned on by default. Follow the steps below to add it to your Drive apps menu.

Opening the Script Editor from your Drive

Click on the 'New' button in Drive then click 'More'.

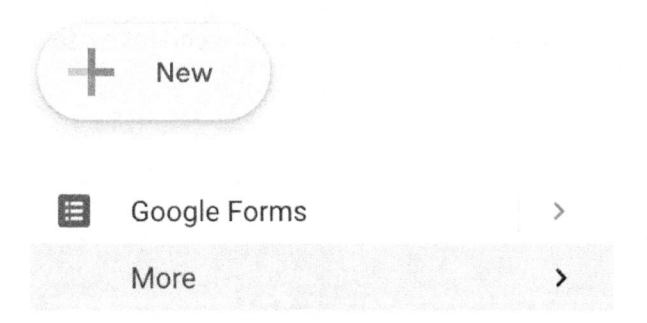

[+ New]

| | Google Forms | > |
| | More | > |

You will see the Google Apps Script app, which is the Script Editor. Click on it to open it.

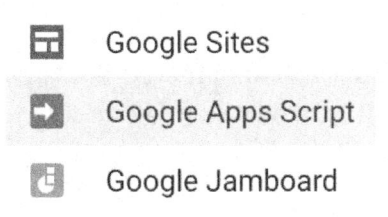

	Google Sites
	Google Apps Script
	Google Jamboard

This will open the Script Editor and there will be an untitled project ready for you to edit.

![Apps Script interface showing Untitled project with Files, Code.gs, Libraries, Services panel and code editor with function myFunction() {}]

Click on 'Untitled project' to rename the file, and type in the name of your script project, then click Rename. It can take a few moments to save.

Rename Project

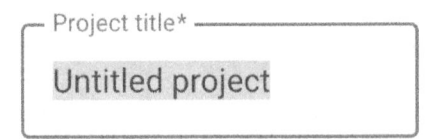

Project title*
Untitled project

Cancel   Rename

Close the Script Editor and you will find its created an Apps Script file in your Drive. This is what's called a standalone script.

ScriptEditor

There are two types of script. The other is a 'bound script', which means it's connected to a particular file. The Script Editor can also be opened within a Google Doc, Sheet, Slides, or Form. When it is, the script is bound to that file.

We'll see in a later chapter an example where we open and edit a script within a form in order to run it from that form.

More information on the Script Editor in **Appendix 2**.

If you're new to JavaScript and Apps Script, in **Appendix 3**, there's information on some of the basic JavaScript areas.

Let's get coding!

1 - Creating files and folders in My Drive

In this chapter, we will start with the basics of creating files and folders. We will look at creating different types of files and creating folders, which will appear in our My Drive.

In the first example, we will see how we authorize a script, as this needs to be done every time we access an Apps Script service.

In the final example, we will see how we can use a loop to make creating multiple files or folders quick and easy to do.

The examples in this book are numbered with the unit number and the example number to help you find what you're looking for, for example, example11 is unit 1, script 1.

So, let's jump right in and create our first file using Apps Script.

Example 11 – Creating a text file

In this example, we're going to create a simple text file in our My Drive.

```
1. //Create a text file
2. function example11() {
3.   DriveApp.createFile("EXAMPLE 11 FILE", "This is a new file");
4. }
```

Line 2: First, create the function called *example11*.

L3: To access our Drive we need to use the **DriveApp** service. Follow this by a dot and **createFile()**.

Here is the information about the **createFile()** method in the Google reference documentation:
https://developers.google.com/apps-script/reference/drive/drive-app#createFile(String,String)

createFile(name, content)

In the brackets, we have 2 parameters. The first is the filename and the second is the content of the file. Put both parts in between single or double quotes. End the line with a semi-colon.

L4: Close the function.

Now, we run the function. From the toolbar, select the example11 function (if not already selected).

example11 ▼

Then click the run button.

▷ Run

Authorizing a script

The first time you run a script or if you use a new service, you have to authorize the script, even if it's just you using it.

13

In this example, we're going to be using the Drive scope as we're going to create a file in our Drive.
Scope:

`https://www.googleapis.com/auth/drive`

When you're first starting out you don't need to worry scopes, except that you will need to authorize the script every time a new one is added.

The process below is the same for all the different scopes you may need to authorize. It's also the same process for anyone who wants to use your script for the first time.

When you run the script, a dialogue box will pop up, stating that authorization is required and the name of the script project that requires it.

1) Click the "Review Permissions" button.

> Authorization required
>
> This project requires your permission to access your data.
>
> Cancel   Review permissions

2) This will ask you to select the account you want the script to access. Usually, you'll just click on the one that appears at the top, as that's the one you ran the script from. If you want to use another, click "Use another account" and select the account you want.

G Sign in with Google

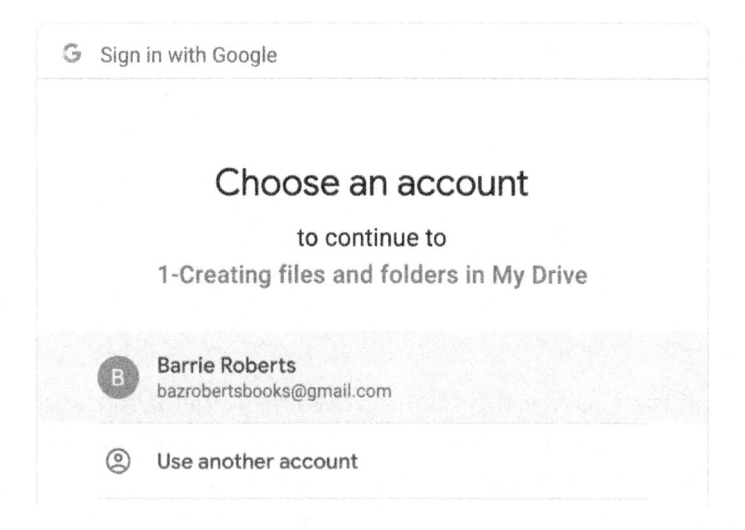

Choose an account

to continue to
1-Creating files and folders in My Drive

Barrie Roberts
bazrobertsbooks@gmail.com

Use another account

3) The "This app isn't verified" message will appear. For all the scripts in this book, you won't need to verify the app. Click "Advanced".

Google hasn't verified this app

The app is requesting access to sensitive info in your Google Account. Until the developer (baz@bazroberts.com) verifies this app with Google, you shouldn't use it.

Advanced   BACK TO SAFETY

4) At the bottom (you may need to scroll down a little), click "Go to 1-Creating files and folders in My Drive (unsafe)". This part

15

always starts with "Go to " + plus the script project name + (unsafe) – which sounds scary but as you're the script writer, it's perfectly safe.

Hide Advanced   BACK TO SAFETY

Continue only if you understand the risks and trust the developer (baz@bazroberts.com).

Go to 1-Creating files and folders in My Drive (unsafe)

5) This will take you to the final part where it will summarize what you want to authorize. It will show the script project name, which account it wants to access, and a summary of what you will allow it to do. Click "Allow" to authorize the script.

If you're using a Google Workspace for Business account, after the Review Permissions screen, you'll be taken straight to this Allow screen.

1-Creating files and folders in My Drive
wants to access your Google Account

B bazrobertsbooks@gmail.com

This will allow
1-Creating files and folders in My Drive **to:**

See, edit, create, and delete all of your Google Drive files

Make sure you trust 1-Creating files and folders in My Drive

You may be sharing sensitive info with this site or app. Learn about how 1-Creating files and folders in My Drive will handle your data by reviewing its terms of service and privacy policies. You can always see or remove access in your Google Account.

Learn about the risks

Cancel   Allow

This will run the script and if we look in our My Drive, we will see a file has been added.

📄 EXAMPLE 11 FILE

Note, you cannot open this type of file directly in Drive but you can download it and open it on your computer. Here, I've opened it and can see the content of the text file.

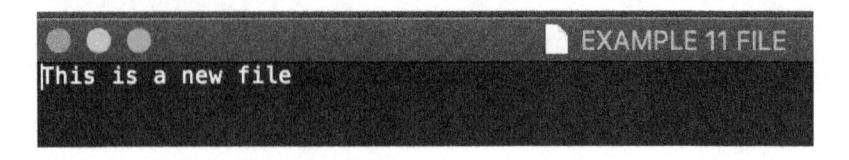

```
This is a new file
```
EXAMPLE 11 FILE

Example 12 – Creating a PDF

There are in fact two **createFile()** methods. The one above has 2 parameters and the one we're going to look at now has three and allows us to state the file type we want.

This time we're going to create a PDF file.

```
6.  //Create a PDF
7.  function example12() {
8.    DriveApp.createFile("EXAMPLE 12 PDF FILE",
9.                        "This is a new PDF file", MimeType.PDF);
10. }
```

L7: The function will be called *example12*.

L8: We use the **DriveApp** service and the **createFile()** method then in the brackets add our 3 parameters. The first two are the same we saw above, i.e. the filename and the content. Then we add the type of file. We write **MimeType** then a dot with the file type. Here it's a PDF.

We then run the function *example12*.

example11 ▼

    example11

    example12

In our My Drive, we can see that a PDF has been created and added.

📄 **EXAMPLE 12 PDF FILE**

Opening the file we can see the text added.

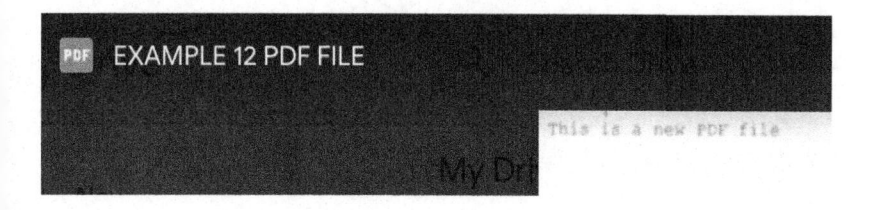

📄 **EXAMPLE 12 PDF FILE**

This is a new PDF file

Example 13 – Creating a new folder

Now, let's create a folder. This is even easier than creating a file, as we only need to name the folder.

```
11.  //Create a new folder
12.  function example13() {
13.     DriveApp.createFolder("EXAMPLE 13
     FOLDER");
14.  }
```

L12: I've named the function *example13*.

L13: We use **DriveApp** again and this time use the **createFolder()** method. In the brackets we add the name of the folder in between quotes.

Run the script and we see it's added a folder in our My Drive with the name we set.

📁 **EXAMPLE 13 FOLDER**

Example 14 – Creating a PDF which contains HTML

Let's go back to creating a file. Above we just added a simple piece in the content part but we can also add HTML in that part to style it better. Here, let's add a simple bit of HTML, where we'll format the text as a header and add italics to one of the words.

```
17.  //Create PDF with HTML
18.  function example14() {
```

```
19.     DriveApp.createFile("EXAMPLE 14 HTML PDF
    FILE",
20.                     "<h1>This is a new
    <em>PDF</em> file</h1>",
21.                     MimeType.PDF);
22. }
```

L18: I've named the function *example14*.

L19: Here we're using the same **createFile()** method as we saw in example 12. In the second part, the content, I've added a simple piece of HTML. In case you don't know HTML tags, this will format the sentence as a header and as a **<h1>** header, i.e. a large one. And wrapped around the word PDF, I've added **<em>** tags to write the word in italics.

Run the script. We can see it's created the PDF as before.

📄   EXAMPLE 14 HTML PDF FILE

Opening it we can see the text is now, much bigger and the word PDF is in italics.

📄 EXAMPLE 14 HTML PDF FILE

This is a new *PDF* file

Example 15 – Creating multiple PDF files

One of the most powerful functions of code is to do multiple actions really quickly. We do that with a loop, which will repeat a piece of code within it a number of times. Here, we're going to create 5 files, each one labelled individually with a consecutive number.

```
24.   //Create multiple PDF files
25.   function example15() {
26.     for(d = 1; d < 6; d++){
27.       DriveApp.createFile("EXAMPLE 15 PDF FILE "+d,
28.         "This is file number "+d, MimeType.PDF);
29.     }
30.   }
```

L25: I've named the function *example15*.

Now we need to set up our loop. There are different types of loop, but the most basic and most common is the **for** loop.

The **for** loop structure is:

for (start value; condition (loop continues while this is true; incremental value each time round the loop) {
  script you want to repeat
}

L26: We start with the keyword **for** and in between the brackets we add the 3 parameters.

First, I'm going to start the counter at 1 and use the variable *d* to keep count (the variable can be named whatever you want, accept for using keywords like **for**).

Next, I want it to keep counting up to 5, so the condition I set is *d* less than 6, so it will keep going until it reaches 5.

In the final part, I want to add 1 to the variable *d*, each time it goes around the loop. We could write *d+=1*, but there is a common short cut to add one, which is to use two pluses after the variable, i.e. *d++.*

Then we use the curly brackets to put what we're going to run within them.

L27: Here, we're going to create the file. To give the file a different name each time we go around the loop, I've added the title as normal then use +*d* to add the number on the variable *d*. So, the first time it will add the number 1, then the next time, the number 2, etc.

L28: I add the content, and again I've added the file number in the text which will match the filename number. Then I add the PDF file type.

L29: Then we close the loop with the curly bracket.

L30: And close the function with a curly bracket.

Run the script.

As you can see it's created 5 PDF files, each named individually.

📄 EXAMPLE 15 PDF FILE 1

📄 EXAMPLE 15 PDF FILE 2

📄 EXAMPLE 15 PDF FILE 3

📄 EXAMPLE 15 PDF FILE 4

📄 EXAMPLE 15 PDF FILE 5

Example 16 – Creating multiple folders

We can also create multiple folders in the same way.

```
32.   //Create multiple folders
33.   function example16() {
34.     for(f = 1; f < 6; f++){
35.       DriveApp.createFolder("EXAMPLE 16 FOLDER NUMBER "+f);
36.     }
37.   }
```

L33: Open the function.

L34: In the loop, let's use the variable *f* to keep count. The rest is the same as the example above.

L35: Use **DriveApp** and **createFolder()** to create a folder. At the end of the folder name, I've added **+f** so that for every folder made it will add a sequential number to identify it.

Run the script.

As you can see it's created 5 folders, each with an individual name.

📁 EXAMPLE 16 FOLDER NUMBER 1

📁 EXAMPLE 16 FOLDER NUMBER 2

📁 EXAMPLE 16 FOLDER NUMBER 3

📁 EXAMPLE 16 FOLDER NUMBER 4

📁 EXAMPLE 16 FOLDER NUMBER 5

2 - Creating files & folders in specific folders

In the previous chapter all the files and folders we created appeared and were stored in our My Drive, i.e. the root folder of Drive but usually we don't want to litter our My Drive with lots of files and folders. Instead we want to have control over where we're going to create the files and folders.

This chapter will show you how to create files and folders within specific folders. It will also introduce you to other methods like getting the folder ID or URL, getting its name, and starring it automatically.

Example 21 – Creating a folder within a folder

Each file and folder has a unique ID which can be used to get it and use it. For folders it's after the /folders/ part in the URL.

```
https://drive.google.com/drive/folders/14g-tIUGinVlMxA77VUZu6TKi5-zXcDdJ
```

If you are trying these examples out for yourself, replace the folder IDs with your own ones.

In this example, we're going to create a folder within a specific folder.

```
1. //Create folder within a folder
2. function example21() {
3.   const folder = DriveApp.getFolderById('14g-tIUGinVlMxA77VUZu6TKi5-zXcDdJ');
```

```
4.    folder.createFolder('EXAMPLE 21 FOLDER');
5. }
```

L2: Set up the function *example21*.

L3: We can get a specific folder by get it by its ID using **DriveApp** and the **getFolderById()** method. In the brackets you paste in the previously copied ID from the URL. Once we get the folder we need to store that information somewhere, and here I'm storing it in a variable (**const**) called *folder*.

L4: Now, I want to create a folder in that folder. So, I type the variable name and use the **createFolder()** method, writing the name of the new folder in the brackets. Notice that instead of using **DriveApp**, which will put the folder in My Drive, we're using the folder we just stored.

Run the function *example21*.

It's added the new folder and it's within the parent folder.

📁 EXAMPLE 21 FOLDER

Example 22 – Creating a file within a folder

Here, we're going to do the same thing with a file.

```
7. //Create file in a folder
8. function example22() {
9.    const folder =
      DriveApp.getFolderById('14g-
      tlUGinVlMxA77VUZu6TKi5-zXcDdJ');
```

27

```
10.    folder.createFile('EXAMPLE 22 FILE',
       'This is a new file.', MimeType.PLAIN_TEXT);
11. }
```

L8: Set up the function.

L9: Get the folder by ID as before and store it in *folder*.

L10: This time we get the folder and then add the **createFile()** method to create the plain text file within the folder.

It's created that file, and it's in that folder.

📄   EXAMPLE 22 FILE

Example 23 – Creating a file in a newly-created folder

Sometimes you don't already have the folder made, so don't have the ID in advance and you want to create the folder, then create a file within that folder. Here let's create a new folder within a folder, then create a text file within that folder.

```
13. //Create file in newly created folder
14. function example23() {
15.    const folder =
       DriveApp.getFolderById('14g-
       tlUGinVlMxA77VUZu6TKi5-zXcDdJ');
16.    const newFolder =
       folder.createFolder('EXAMPLE 23 SUB
       FOLDER');
17.    newFolder.createFile('EXAMPLE 23 FILE',
       'This is a new file.', MimeType.PLAIN_TEXT);
18. }
```

L14: Set up the function.

L15: Get the parent folder by its ID.

L16: Create a folder within the parent folder and give it a name. This time store that newly-created folder in the variable called *newFolder*. This will then allow you to refer to and work with that folder.

L17: Now I get that new folder and create a plain text file within it.

L18: Close the function.

Run the script.

As you can see, it's created the folder called "EXAMPLE 23 SUB FOLDER" within the parent folder.

📁　EXAMPLE 23 SUB FOLDER

When we open that folder we will see that it has created the text file within it.

📄　EXAMPLE 23 FILE

29

Example 24 – Creating a new folder, getting its URL and name, starring it, and creating a new file within it

Here we're going to look at other methods related to folders and you will see how easy it is to get a variety of information and to then use that information later on.

We're going to create a folder within a folder, then get its URL and name, and then star it. Then we'll create a file, which will use the folder name we previously obtained and add the folder URL within the document.

```
20. //Get URL and name of new folder, star it,
    add URL in text file
21. function example24() {
22.   const folder =
   DriveApp.getFolderById('14g-
   tlUGinVlMxA77VUZu6TKi5-zXcDdJ');
23.   const newFolder =
   folder.createFolder('EXAMPLE 24 SUB
   FOLDER');
24.   const newFolderUrl = newFolder.getUrl();
25.   const newFolderName =
   newFolder.getName();
26.   newFolder.setStarred(true);
27.   newFolder.createFile(newFolderName,
28.     "New folder URL: "+newFolderUrl,
29.     MimeType.PLAIN_TEXT);
30. }
```

L21: Set up the function

L22: Get the parent folder by its ID.

L23: Create a folder within the parent folder and store it in the variable called *newFolder*.

L24: Get the new folder's URL by using the **getUrl()** method on *newFolder*. Store it in the variable *newFolderUrl*.

L25: Get the new folder's name by using the **getName()** method and store it in the variable *newFolderName*.

L26: Now, let's star our new folder by using the **setStarred()** method and passing *true* in the brackets. False would remove a star.

L27: Create a new file in the new folder. For its name, use the variable *newFolderName*.

L28: In the content, let's add the new folder's URL using the variable *newFolderUrl*. Note, how we combine text and a variable or variable together. The text is in quotes and the variable is added with a plus sign.

L29: The file will a plain text file.

Note, lines 27 to 29 were written on different lines, just to reduce the width of the code.

L30: Close the function.

Run the script.

As we can see it's created the folder.

EXAMPLE 24 SUB FOLDER ★

31

And the text file.

📄 EXAMPLE 24 SUB FOLDER

Opening the file, we will see that the text has been added along with the folder's URL.

```
EXAMPLE 24 SUB FOLDER         Open with Google Docs
    New folder URL: https://drive.google.com/drive/folders/19n3FTjthrZYC6VID74AkoPKt-LT97gxk
```

Note, you can open a text file as a Google Doc by clicking on "Open with Google Docs" from the text file viewer. This creates a new Google Doc file with the text file info.

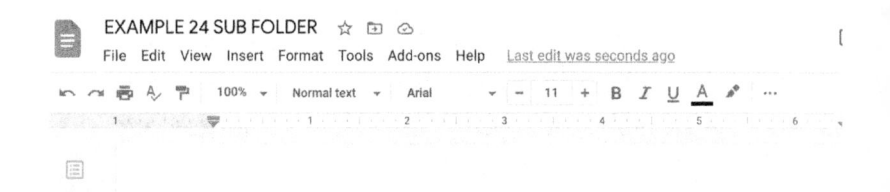

```
EXAMPLE 24 SUB FOLDER  ☆
File  Edit  View  Insert  Format  Tools  Add-ons  Help   Last edit was seconds ago
        100%    Normal text    Arial    -  11  +  B  I  U  A

New folder URL: https://drive.google.com/drive/folders/19n3FTjthrZYC6VID74AkoPKt-LT97gxk
```

Example 24b – Chaining methods and variables

We can write the above code in a slightly different way, to reduce the amount written.

```
32.  //Get URL and name of new folder, star it,
     add URL in text file (linked const &
     chaining)
33.  function example24b() {
34.    const folder =
     DriveApp.getFolderById('14g-
     tlUGinVlMxA77VUZu6TKi5-zXcDdJ'),
```

```
35.        newFolder = 
   folder.createFolder('EXAMPLE 24 SUB 
   FOLDER'),
36.         newFolderUrl = newFolder.getUrl(),
37.         newFolderName = newFolder.getName();
38.     newFolder.setStarred(true)
39.               .createFile(newFolderName,
40.               "New folder URL: 
   "+newFolderUrl,
41.        MimeType.PLAIN_TEXT);
42. }
```

L34-37: Here, instead of typing **const** for every line, we can use just one **const** and then chain them together by using a comma and not a semi-colon at the end of each statement, except the last one. It can lead to slightly cleaner looking, less busy code, but if you have to edit any of the variables it can be a bit of a pain.

Personally, if first starting off I would stick to the previous example and use **const** every time, partly to make it clear to you what's happening on every line, and often you're thinking about what's happening in the code line-by-line, so won't be thinking of it in terms of groups at a time.

That said, you may see code written like this and it's important to know that it does the same thing.

L38-41: Here, I've also chained the method, **createFile()** to the one above **setStarred()**. This meant that I didn't have to type out *newFolder* again.
Plus, it shows the two are connected together, and leads to cleaner looking code. Note, that there is no semi-colon after the

setStarred() method. Again, starting off you may wish to stick to the previous style first.

3 – Making copies of files and creating folders from a URL

So far, we've looked at creating new files and folders. In this chapter we're going to look at:

- How to make copies of files
- How to create a folder from a URL stored in a Google Sheet
- How to call a function from within another function
- How we can return content back to our original function
- How to extract a file or folder ID from a URL

Note, I've shortened the IDs used in the examples, to reduce the width of the code so it's easier to read on the page. As always, replace these IDs with your own ones.

Example 31 – Making a copy of a file

Here we're going to get a master file by its ID and then make a copy of it and place it in a specific folder.

📄　Master document

The contents of the document look like this:

35

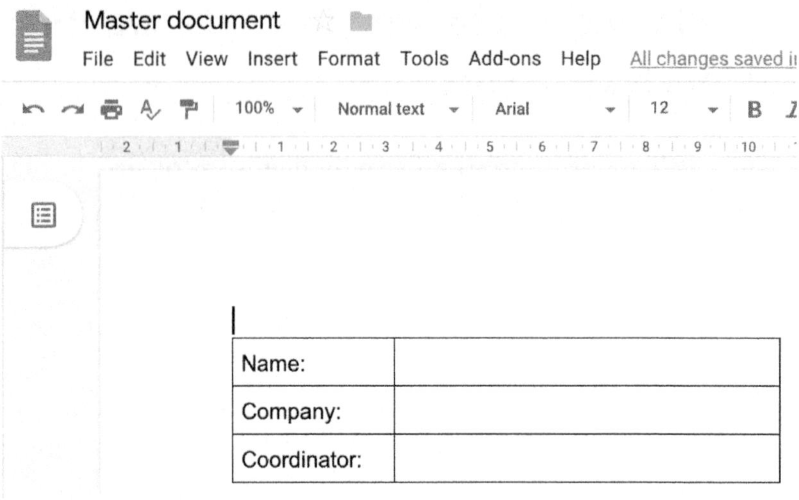


```
1. //Make copy of file
2. function example31() {
3.   const folder =
   DriveApp.getFolderById('14g-
   tlUGinVlMxA77VUZu6TKi5-zXcDdJ');
4.   const masterFile =
   DriveApp.getFileById('15UR9rxKfHcJb0Ws7VaIFG
   gJ2eqov2o5OwJY7nm2fnR8');
5.   masterFile.makeCopy("EXAMPLE 31 DOCUMENT",
   folder);
6. }
```

L2: Set up the function

L3: Let’s get the folder we’re going to place our file into, by getting it by its ID and storing that in the variable *folder*.

L4: Now let’s get the master file by its ID and store it in the variable *masterFile*.

L5: Now we get the master file and use the **makeCopy()** method to do just that, make a copy. In the brackets, there are 2 parameters. The first is the new filename and the second is the destination of the file, i.e. where you're going to store it. Here, we add the folder we have stored in the variable *folder*.

L6: We close the function.

Run the function.

As we can see, it's created a new document called "EXAMPLE 31 DOCUMENT".

📄 EXAMPLE 31 DOCUMENT

And we can see that the content is the same as the master one.

EXAMPLE 31 DOCUMENT

Name:	
Company:	
Coordinator:	

Example 32 – Getting a file URL stored in a Sheet, extracting the ID, and making a copy of the file

Here we're going to make a copy of file but this time we're going to get the file URL which is stored in a Google Sheet, then extract the file ID from it, so we can then make a copy of it.

This is useful where you have users that you don't want them to have access to the code, or indeed just don't want them to have to worry about how it works, they just add the URL in the Google Sheet and run the script from there.

Plus, sometimes there are cases where you only have the URL to work with and you need to get the ID in order to make the copy.

We're also going to see how we call another function from within a function and how we return some information back to our function.

```
8.  //Get file URL in sheet, get ID from it, make copy of file
9.  function example32() {
10.     const folder = DriveApp.getFolderById('14g-tlUGinVlMxA77VUZu6TKi5-zXcDdJ');
11.     var fileId = convertFileUrlToId();
12.     Logger.log(fileId);
13.     const masterFile = DriveApp.getFileById(fileId);
14.     masterFile.makeCopy("EXAMPLE 32 DOCUMENT", folder);
15. }
```

L9: Setup the first function called *example32*.

L10: Get the folder we're going to put the file into.

L11: This is where we're going to call another function, in this case, called *convertFileUrlToId*. Write the name of the function then follow it by a pair of normal brackets and a semi-colon.

We're going to be receiving some information back from that function, so we need a place to store it, which will be in a variable called *fileId*.

In this example, we could have used a constant variable, I often use this set up if the second function is being run multiple times, and therefore, the information coming back is different each time and a constant variable wouldn't work.

L12: I've only added this line to show you what is returned from the other function. Here it will log the file ID that is returned by the second function.

L13: Now, we use that file ID to get the file and store it in the variable *masterFile*.

L14: We then make a copy of the master file and place it in our folder.

L15: We close the function.

So, what's going on in the other function? This is the part that will get the file URL from the Sheet and extract the file ID from it.

Here's the URL we want to use:

	A
1	https://docs.google.com/document/d/15UR9rxKfHcJb0Ws7ValFGgJ2eqov2o5OwJY7nm2fnR8/edit

Underneath the above function we write this one:

```
17.  //Get File URL stored in spreadsheet, getID
     from it using replace
18.  function convertFileUrlToId() {
19.    const ss =
       SpreadsheetApp.openById('1dbjCPQbu99MKR59aff
       Lr1JHVNXzX0bsdxLvBZV94r2A');
20.    const sheet =
       ss.getSheetByName('Sheet1');
21.    const fileUrl =
       sheet.getRange(1,1).getValue();
22.    var fileId =
       fileUrl.replace("https://docs.google.com/doc
       ument/d/", "");
23.    var fileId = fileId.replace("/edit", "");
24.    return fileId;
25.  }
```

L18: Set up the second function called *convertFileUrlToId*.

To get the URL in the spreadsheet, we will need to get the spreadsheet, then get the sheet it's on, then get the cell it's in and finally, get the value in that cell.

L19: We need to get the Google Sheet, so we use a different service called **SpreadsheetApp** and open that file by its ID. Then we store the spreadsheet in the variable called *ss*.

L20: We then need to get the sheet we need, which in this case is called "Sheet1". To do so, we use the variable *ss* and get the sheet by its name. Then we store that in the variable called *sheet*.

L21: The URL is stored in cell A1, so we get the range 1,1 (row 1, column 1), and get its value. We then store that in the variable *fileUrl*.

So, now we have the file URL.

L22: Now, we need to extract the ID from the URL. To do so, we'll use the method **replace()**. This replaces a string with another string. We use the **replace()** method on the *fileUrl* variable and in the brackets we state the text we want to replace, which first will be the start of the URL up to where the ID starts.

|◄--------| |--------►|
https://docs.google.com/document/d/15UR9rxKfHcJb0Ws7VaIFGgJ2eqov2o5OwJY7nm2fnR8/edit

In the second parameter we state what the replacement will be and in this case, it's nothing, so we just add a pair of quotes. We store the result in the variable *fileId*.

L23: That has removed the first part of the URL, but now we need to remove the last part "/edit". So, we use the replace method again and this time replace the edit part. Again we add it to the variable *fileId*, which will update it and which will now contain just the file ID.

41

L24: We need to return this ID back to our original function. To do so, we use the keyword **return** and state the variable we're returning, followed by a semi-colon.

L25: We close the function.

Run the function *example32*.

As we can see, it's created a copy of our master and named it.

📄 EXAMPLE 32 DOCUMENT

In the execution log, we can see the file ID that has been extracted:

Execution log

```
1:24:03 PM    Notice    Execution started
1:24:04 PM    Info      15UR9rxKfHcJb0Ws7VaIFGgJ2eqov2o5OwJY7nm2fnR8
```

As we can see, it had logged just the file ID, showing that the file ID had been returned from our second function and received correctly in the first one.

We could have written the above code all in one function, but there are times where you want to separate out part of your code, usually because this part does a specific function and possibly because you want to run that function again later in the code, so you call it again instead of having to write it again.

This is more relevant to longer codes but as we've seen above, we can group our programs into different functions, which can make them easier to understand and to correct and update.

Plus, of course the main reason here was to show you how to do it.

Example 33 – Getting a folder URL stored in a Sheet, extracting the ID, and creating a folder in that folder

We're going to do something very similar to the above but this time with a folder. We're not going to copy a folder (partly because these isn't a method for that), we're going to use the ID we extract from the URL and to then be able to create a folder within another folder.

```
27.  //Get folder URL in sheet, get ID from it,
     create new folder using ID
28.  function example33() {
29.    var folderId = convertFolderUrlToId();
30.    Logger.log(folderId);
31.    const mainFolder =
       DriveApp.getFolderById(folderId);
32.    mainFolder.createFolder("EXAMPLE33 - NEW
       SUB FOLDER");
33.  }
```

L28: Set up the first function called *example33*.

L29: Here we're going to catch the output from the function called *convertFolderUrlToId* and store it in the variable *folderId*.

L30: We'll log the folder ID like we did before with the file one.

L31: We then get the folder by that ID and store it in the variable *mainFolder*.

L32: We then create a new folder in that main folder and give it a name.

L33: Close the function.

We're going to use the same Google Sheet as the previous example and the folder URL is in cell A2.

	A
1	https://docs.google.com/document/d/15UR9rxKfHcJb0Ws7ValFGgJ2eqov2o5OwJY7nm2fnR8/edit
2	https://drive.google.com/drive/folders/14g-tIUGinVIMxA77VUZu6TKi5-zXcDdJ

Underneath the above function write the following:

```
35.    //Get Folder URL stored in spreadsheet,
       getID from it using replace
36.    function convertFolderUrlToId() {
37.        const ss =
       SpreadsheetApp.openById('1dbjCPQbu99MKR59aff
       Lr1JHVNXzX0bsdxLvBZV94r2A');
38.        const sheet =
       ss.getSheetByName('Sheet1');
39.        const folderUrl =
       sheet.getRange(2,1).getValue();
40.        const folderId =
       folderUrl.replace("https://drive.google.com/
       drive/folders/", "");
41.        return folderId;
42.    }
```

L36: Set up the function called *convertFolderUrlToId*.

L37-38: The same as before, we get the spreadsheet and get the sheet called *Sheet1*.

L39: We get the value in cell A2, so write in the range 2,1 (row 2, column 1) and store it in the variable *folderUrl*.

L40: The folder URL is a little easier to extract as we only have to remove the first part. We use the **replace()** method again to remove the part before the ID.

https://drive.google.com/drive/folders/14g-tIUGinVIMxA77VUZu6TKi5-zXcDdJ

L41: We return the folder ID.

L42: Close the function.

Run the function *example33*.

As we can see, it's created a new folder in our parent folder.

EXAMPLE33 - NEW SUB FOLDER

We can also see in the log that it has extracted the ID correctly.

Example 34 – Alternative way to extract the file ID from a file URL

As a little extra, here we're going to have a quick look at how we can extract the file ID from the file URL, this time using a regular expression. A regular expression is a sequence of characters which define a search pattern. If you want to know

45

more about these, I'd recommend you go to this W3schools page: https://www.w3schools.com/js/js_regexp.asp
Our first function is basically the same as *example32*.

```
44.  //Get file URL in sheet, get ID from it,
     make copy of file
45.  function example34() {
46.    const folder =
     DriveApp.getFolderById('14g-
     tlUGinVlMxA77VUZu6TKi5-zXcDdJ');
47.    var fileId = convertFileUrlToId2();
48.    const masterFile =
     DriveApp.getFileById(fileId);
49.    masterFile.makeCopy("EXAMPLE 34
     DOCUMENT", folder);
50.  }
```

The second one is the same except we not going to use the **replace()** method, instead in line 57 we're going to use the **match()** method.

```
52.  //Get File URL stored in spreadsheet, getID
     from it using Regular Expression
53.  function convertFileUrlToId2() {
54.    const ss =
     SpreadsheetApp.openById('1dbjCPQbu99MKR59aff
     Lr1JHVNXzX0bsdxLvBZV94r2A');
55.    const sheet =
     ss.getSheetByName('Sheet1');
56.    const fileUrl =
     sheet.getRange(1,1).getValue();
57.    var fileId = fileUrl.match(/[-\w]{25,}/);
58.    Logger.log(fileId);
59.    return fileId;
60.  }
```

Here's line 57 closer up:

```
var fileId = fileUrl.match(/[-\w]{25,}/);
```

We get the file URL and add the **match()** method to it. The regular expression is in between the brackets and is highlighted in red. I'm not going to explain how it works exactly, as it's beyond the scope of this book, but the important thing is that it extracts the ID part from the URL.

The Internet is full of expressions like this which can do some amazing things and all you have to do is copy and paste them into your code.

4 – Moving files and folders and adding shortcuts

In this chapter, we'll look at how we can move files and folders to different folders, and also how we can add shortcuts to files or folders in other folders.

At the end of 2020, Google removed the possibility of having files and folders in more than one place and replaced it with making shortcuts to the original file and folder. So, even though a file or folder is only in one location, we can create a shortcut to that location in a different folder.

We'll look at:

- How to move a file and a folder to a different folder, whether this is in a folder or recently-created in My Drive
- How to create a shortcut in one folder to another folder (or file)

If you are trying out these examples, please replace the file and folder IDs with your own as otherwise either the scripts won't work or you won't have access to the folders.

Example 41 – Move a file and a folder from one folder to another

Here we'll create two folders and a file in a parent folder. Then we'll move the file to the second folder, and then the first newly-created folder to the second folder too.

```
1.  //Create 2 folders and file in parent
    folder, move file & folder1 to folder2
2.  function example41() {
3.    const parentFolder =
      DriveApp.getFolderById('14g-
      tlUGinVlMxA77VUZu6TKi5-zXcDdJ');
4.    const folder1 =
      parentFolder.createFolder("EXAMPLE41-
      FOLDER1");
5.    const folder2 =
      parentFolder.createFolder("EXAMPLE41-
      FOLDER2");
6.    const file =
      parentFolder.createFile("EXAMPLE41-NEW
      FILE",
7.          "This file has moved from one folder
      to another.",
8.          MimeType.PLAIN_TEXT);
9.    file.moveTo(folder2);
10.   folder1.moveTo(folder2);
11. }
```

L2: Set up the function.

L3: Get the parent folder by its ID.

L4: Create folder1 within that folder, and store it in the variable *folder1*.

L5: Create folder2 within the parent folder, and store it in the variable *folder2*.

L6-8: Create the text file in the parent folder.

L9: Use the **moveTo()** method to move the file from the parent folder to *folder2*.

L10: Move folder1 to folder2, again using the **moveTo()** method.

Note, we wouldn't normally create a file or folder in one folder then move it to another, we would just create them in the folder we want to them to end up in.

Example 42 – Move a file from My Drive to a specific folder

In this example, we're going to create a Google Doc which will be in our My Drive then move it to a specific folder. It shows you that you can move files and folders from My Drive as well as specific folders.

```
13.  //Make Google Doc, move from My Drive to
     folder
14.  function example42() {
15.     var newDoc =
     DocumentApp.create("EXAMPLE42-New Google
     Doc");
16.     var newDoc =
     DriveApp.getFileById(newDoc.getId());
17.     const parentFolder =
     DriveApp.getFolderById('14g-
     tlUGinVlMxA77VUZu6TKi5-zXcDdJ');
18.     newDoc.moveTo(parentFolder);
19.  }
```

L14: Set up the function.

L15: Create the Google Doc using the **DocumentApp** and the **create()** method.

L16: To move the Doc we need to first get it by its ID. So we use the **DriveApp** and use the **getFileById()** method to get it.

L17: We're going to move it into the parent folder, so first we get that by its ID.

L18: To move the file, we use the file and then the **moveTo()** method, putting the new folder in the brackets.

Example 43 – Remove a folder from a folder

Here we're going to remove a file or folder from a specific folder. When it's removed it is placed in your My Drive.

```
21. //Get 2 folders by their IDs and remove one
    folder from within the other one
22. function example43() {
23.   const parentFolder =
      DriveApp.getFolderById('14g-
      tlUGinVlMxA77VUZu6TKi5-zXcDdJ');
24.   const folder =
      parentFolder.createFolder("EXAMPLE43-
      FOLDER");
25.   parentFolder.removeFolder(folder);
26. }
```

L22: Set up the function.

L23: Get the folder you want to remove the file or folder from by its ID.

L24: Let's create a folder in that folder, which we will then remove. This line you wouldn't normally have, it's just to create a folder to then use.

L25: We then use the **removeFolder()** method to remove the folder.

If you go to your My Drive, you will see the folder is now there.

Note, to remove a file just use **removeFile()** instead of **removeFolder()** having gotten the file by its ID previously.

Example 44 – Add shortcut in a specific folder to a file or folder

In the next example, we're going to use the Drive API and this needs to be turned on in the Advanced Google Services.

In the editor, click on the plus button next to Services.

Services   +

Then scroll down the list until you find Drive API. Select that then click Add.

Content API for Shopping

Drive API   Documentation

Drive Activity API

Add

Back in the editor, you'll see the Drive service has been added.

Services   +

Drive

📁 Google Apps Script BOOKS

In case you don't already now, if you right-click on a file or folder, you can create a shortcut to it and state where that shortcut is.

△+ Add a shortcut to Drive

So, you can quickly access that file or folder from wherever you decide on your Drive, which is really useful, and can save you going in and out of multiple folders to get to where you want.

Let's see how we can add a shortcut automatically.

Here, we're going to get a folder, then, create a shortcut in it to a Google Slides presentation on our Drive. The type of file is irrelevant and this works for making shortcuts to folders as well, as it uses file or folder IDs as we saw in the previous examples.

```
28. //Add shortcut in a specific folder to a
    file located in another
29. function example44() {
```

53

```
30.     const folderCreateSCin =
   DriveApp.getFolderById('14g-
   tlUGinVlMxA77VUZu6TKi5-zXcDdJ');
31.     const fileToLinkTo =
   DriveApp.getFileById('15o7kOAFY5gHthY46xGA7Q
   UGEGCFczb-qaLYY_sf3iRU');
32.     const folderId =
   folderCreateSCin.getId();
33.     const targetId = fileToLinkTo.getId();
34.
35.     const shortcutName = "NEW SHORTCUT-To
   File 'Weekly Presentation'",
36.        resource = {
37.           shortcutDetails: { targetId: targetId
   },
38.           title: shortcutName,
39.           mimeType: "application/vnd.google-
   apps.shortcut",
40.        };
41.
42.     if (folderId) resource.parents = [{ id:
   folderId }];
43.     Drive.Files.insert(resource);
44. }
```

L29: Open the function.

L30: Get the folder you want to add the shortcut in.

L31: Get the file or folder you want to link to.

L32-33: Get the IDs of the folder and the file.

L35: State the name you want to add to the shortcut.

L36: Now, we need to set up the "resource" all wrapped up in curly brackets.

L37: This consists of the *shortcutDetails*, which needs the ID of the file or folder you're linking to.

L38: The *title* of the shortcut, i.e. the shortcut name.

L39-40: Set the *mimeType* it is, which in this case is a Google Apps shortcut, so we add "application/vnd.google-apps.shortcut". Then close the resource object.

L42: We do a quick check the folder ID is present and if it is we set the **resource.parents** to the folder ID.

L43: Finally, we insert our shortcut, using the contents of the resource we set up.

Run the script and you'll see a new shortcut added.

NEW SHORTCUT-To File 'Weekly Presentation'

This works the same for both files and folders.

You can find more information about the Drive API here:
https://developers.google.com/apps-script/advanced/drive

https://developers.google.com/drive/api/v2/about-files

5 – Adding and removing editors to/from files & folders

After creating files and folders, it's sometimes important to control who has access to them. In this chapter, we're going to look at:

- How we can add specific editors to our files and folders and how to remove them.
- How to stop editors being able to share files or folders.
- How to give only view access to a folder.
- How to share a folder giving anyone with a link edit access.

Example 51 – Adding an editor to a newly-created folder

Here we'll create a new folder and then add a new editor to it.

```
1. //Add editor to folder
2. function example51() {
3.   const folder = DriveApp.createFolder("EXAMPLE51");
4.   folder.addEditor('brgablog@gmail.com');
5. }
```

L2: Set up the function.

L3: Create a new folder and store it in the variable *folder*.

L4: To add an editor to the folder we use the **addEditor()** method and in the brackets write the user's email address within quotes.

L5: Close the function.

We see it creates the new folder in our My Drive and you can see from the person icon it's been shared.

📁 EXAMPLE51

Opening the sharing settings, we can see it's now shared with the owner and my alter ego Baz Roberts.

Share with people and groups

Add people and groups

Barrie Roberts (you)
bazrobertsbooks@gmail.com — Owner

Baz Roberts
brgablog@gmail.com — Editor ▾

Note, if you create a folder within an already existing folder, then the new folder will assume the sharing rights of the parent folder by default.

This is one reason why you might want to control the access, as you may have a parent folder which you don't want to share with everyone, but a specific folder within it you do.

Example 52 – Adding multiple editors and not allowing them to share the folder

Adding multiple editors one-by-one would be a real pain but of course there's a quick way to add more than one user. In this example we'll look at that and how we can also stop them from sharing the folder with others.

```
7.  //Add editors to folder & don't allow them
    to share it
8.  function example52() {
9.    const folder =
    DriveApp.createFolder("EXAMPLE52");
10.     folder.addEditors(['brgablog@gmail.com',
11.
    'roberts.barrie@gmail.com']);
12.     folder.setShareableByEditors(false);
13. }
```

L8: Set up the function.

L9: Create a folder.

L10-11: To add multiple editors, we first need to use the **addEditors()** method, note the plural, and then in the brackets we add an array of email addresses.

An array is in between square brackets and each item in that array is separated with a comma. The email addresses need to be in quotes as before, as the method expects string values.

L12: Now let's make sure they can't share the folder with anyone else. We do this with the **setShareableByEditors()** method. This expects two possible values, *true* if we want them to be able to share the folder, and *false* if we don't. So, this case it's *false*. This is what is known as a Boolean value (true or false).

L13: Close the function.

As we can see it creates the new folder.

EXAMPLE52

Opening the sharing settings, we can see that it's shared the folder with the 2 users.

Share with people and groups

Add people and groups

Barrie Roberts (you) bazrobertsbooks@gmail.com	Owner
Barrie Roberts roberts.barrie@gmail.com	Editor ▾
Baz Roberts brgablog@gmail.com	Editor ▾

Click on the settings cog icon.

We can see the "Editors can change permissions and share" is unchecked, thus preventing the editors from changing access and sharing with people.

← **Share with people settings**

☐ Editors can change permissions and share

Example 53 – Removing an editor from a file

The opposite of adding editors is removing them and we can do that in a similar way. In this example we're going to add a couple of editors, then remove one.

I wouldn't normally do this, as normally we would just be removing the editor, but this is just to make sure our folder has a couple of editors, so I can remove one to show how it's done.

```
15.   //Remove editor from folder
16.   function example53() {
17.     const folder =
      DriveApp.createFolder("EXAMPLE53");
18.     folder.addEditors(['brgablog@gmail.com',
19.
       'roberts.barrie@gmail.com']);
20.
       folder.removeEditor('brgablog@gmail.com');
21.   }
```

L16: Set up the function.

L17: Create a folder.

L18-19: Add 2 editors.

Incidentally, I've put the second email address on a separate line, to reduce the width of the code, so that it fits on the page better.

L20: Now, we're going to remove one of the editors by using the **removeEditor()** method.

L21: Close the function.

Click on the newly-created folder and open the sharing settings.

EXAMPLE53

We can see that we are left with just the one new editor (apart from the owner of course). Obviously, normally we wouldn't add someone, then remove them.

Barrie Roberts (you)
bazrobertsbooks@gmail.com

Barrie Roberts
roberts.barrie@gmail.com

Example 54 – Giving view access to a folder to a user

It's not just edit access we can give, we can also give a user just view access.

```
23.   //Add viewer to folder
24.   function example54() {
25.     const folder =
      DriveApp.createFolder("EXAMPLE54");
```

61

```
26.      folder.addViewer('brgablog@gmail.com');
27.    }
```

L24: Set up the function.

L25: Create a folder.

L26: This time instead of **addEditor()** we use the **addViewer()** method.

L27: Close the function.

Click on the newly-created folder and open the sharing settings.

EXAMPLE54

As you can see, Baz Roberts has view access only.

Barrie Roberts (you)
bazrobertsbooks@gmail.com   Owner

Baz Roberts
brgablog@gmail.com   Viewer

As with **addEditors()** we can multiple users with **addViewers()**.

Example 55 – Giving anyone with link edit access to a folder

In this final example, we'll see how we can share a folder not just with specific users but give access to anyone with the link and how we can control that access, in this case giving them edit access.

Doing it manually in the sharing settings, you would have two options, share with anyone with the link, or restrict it to sharing with specific people.

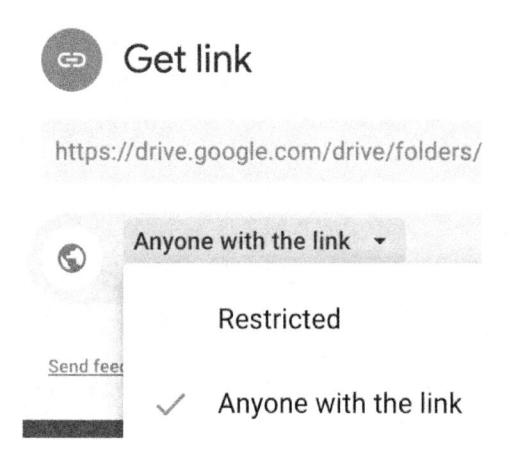

Get link

https://drive.google.com/drive/folders/

Anyone with the link ▼

Restricted

✓ Anyone with the link

To give anyone with the link access, we would select the "Anyone with the link" option.

Here, we can also change the permissions for that file or folder, by giving them viewer, commenter, or editor rights.

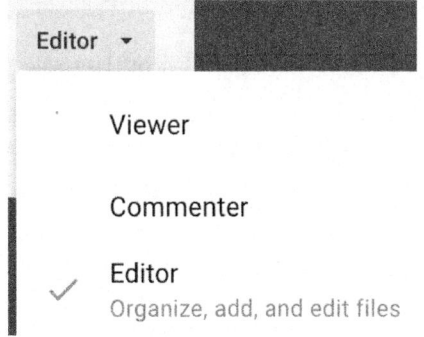

Editor ▼

Viewer

Commenter

✓ Editor
Organize, add, and edit files

Let's see how we do it in the script.

63

```
29.   //Set access to Anyone with a link, and
      with Edit rights
30.   function example55() {
31.     const folder =
      DriveApp.createFolder("EXAMPLE55");
32.
      folder.setSharing(DriveApp.Access.ANYONE_WIT
      H_LINK,
33.     DriveApp.Permission.EDIT);
34.   }
```

L30: Set up the function.

L31: Create a folder.

L32: Here instead of adding editors or viewers, we need to set the sharing status. We do that by using the **setSharing()** method, which then needs two parameters. The first is what type of access you want to give them. I.e. who you're giving access to.

L33: The second part we need to set the permissions, i.e. what type of access to give them.

So, we again use the **DriveApp** to get the permission, then set it, in this case as "edit".

L34: Close the function.

Click on the newly-created folder and open the share settings.

EXAMPLE55

As we can see it's given access to anyone with the link and given them edit permission.

🔗 Get link

Anyone on the internet with this link can edit (sign in required)
Change

There are more options to control access and permissions and even ownership of the files and folders. For more info go to the Google documentation:

https://developers.google.com/apps-script/reference/drive/folder#setsharingaccesstype-permissiontype

https://developers.google.com/apps-script/reference/drive/access

https://developers.google.com/apps-script/reference/drive/permission

6 – Copying a Doc and making a PDF from it

In this chapter, we're going bring some of the different methods we've looked at so far together, like **getFileById()**, **makeCopy()**, **getId()**, **addFile()**, **getName()**, etc.

In the first example we'll:

- make a copy of a master Google Doc
- create a PDF file
- move it to a specific folder
- and delete the original copy of the Google Doc.

The second example will look at how we can quickly and easily create a map, using the same principle as we use for creating the PDF.

Example 61 – Copying a Doc, creating a PDF from it, moving it to a folder, deleting the copied Google Doc

I'll break the script down into 3 parts. First, we need to make a copy of the master document.

Master document

This document contains a simple table ready to be filled out.

Master document

Name:	
Company:	
Coordinator:	

```
1. //Convert Doc to PDF
2. function example61() {
3.   //Make copy of Doc
4.   const masterDoc = DriveApp.getFileById('15UR9rxKfHcJb0Ws7Va-nm2fnR8');
5.   const newDoc = masterDoc.makeCopy("EXAMPLE 61 - Company document");
6.   const newDocId = newDoc.getId();
```

L2: Set up the function.

L4: Get the master document by its ID and store it in the variable *masterDoc*.

L5: Make a copy of the master, name it and store it in the variable *newDoc*.

L6: Get the ID of the new document and store it in *newDocId*.

Now, let's create a PDF from the Google Doc we've just made.

```
8.     //create a PDF file from this Doc
9.     const pdf =
   DriveApp.getFileById(newDocId).getAs('applic
   ation/pdf');
10.      pdf.setName(newDoc.getName() + ".pdf");
11.      const docPdf = DriveApp.createFile(pdf);
```

L9: To create a PDF of our Doc, we first need to get the Doc by its ID and then get it as a PDF using 'application/pdf'. Then store that information in the variable *pdf*.

Note, this is raw data about the file. If we log *pdf* at this point, we will see it's called a 'blob'. A brilliant name, which basically means it acts like a file and contains raw data, which we can use later on.

Info   Blob

L10: Next, let's give a name to this file. Here I'm going to use the same name I gave the copy of the Google Doc, i.e. "EXAMPLE 61 – Company document". To do that, we just use the **getName()** method on the *newDoc* variable, then I add the file format .pdf.

L11: Now we create the file from the blob stored in *pdf*. We do that with the **createFile()** method and pass the *pdf* blob in the brackets. Let's store it in a variable, *docPDF*, so we can move it.

Finally, let's move the PDF into the folder we want and remove it from My Drive and delete the Google Doc also in My Drive.

```
13.     //Add a copy of pdf in doc folder, delete
        original pdf, & delete orig Doc
14.     const folder =
        DriveApp.getFolderById('14g-
        tlUGinVlMxA77VUZu6TKi5-zXcDdJ');
15.     docPdf.moveTo(folder);
16.
        DriveApp.getFileById(newDocId).setTrashed(tr
        ue);
17.   }
```

L14: Get the folder we want by its ID and store it in *folder*.

L15: Get the PDF document and use **moveTo()** to move it to the new folder.

L16: To delete the original Google Doc, we need to get it by its ID then we set it as 'trashed', which means it will be moved to the trash/bin. *True* means it's trashed, *false* would mean it's not.

L17: Close the function.

Run the script and we can see it's made a copy of our master document and made a PDF version of it and it's in the folder we want and not on My Drive.

📄 EXAMPLE 61 - Company document.pdf

Opening we can see it's the same as our original master.

69

Name:	
Company:	
Coordinator:	

I hope you can see that will a little bit of code you can quickly create a PDF document you want, in a place you want it.

Example 62 – Creating a map

Blobs aren't just useful for making PDFs, raw data can be captured for other uses. Here I'm going to quickly show how you can use a blob to store Google map data to then be able to produce an image of that map.

```
20.   //Create image of a map
21.   function example62() {
22.     const map =
      Maps.newStaticMap().setCenter('Chepstow
      castle, Chepstow, UK');
23.     DriveApp.createFile(map);
24.   }
```

L21: Set up the function.

We're going to use the **Maps** service. Like Drive, this is one of the basic Apps Script services available. I want to show you how easy it is to make one using data stored in a blob from the **Maps** service, then add the image it to your My Drive.

L22: We start with the **Maps** service, then use the **newStaticMap()** method to make our map. Then we state where in the world we want the map to centre on, using the **setCenter()** method. Then we add the address we want. We then store this data in the variable *map*.

Note, the address needs to be detailed or individual enough so that Google Maps can find it.

L23: Then using **DriveApp** we create a file using the blob stored in *map*, which will appear in My Drive.

L24: Close the function.

Run the script and in your My Drive, you will have an image file (.png) of our map.

map.png

Open the image and you'll see your map, in this case of a castle in a beautiful town in Wales called Chepstow.

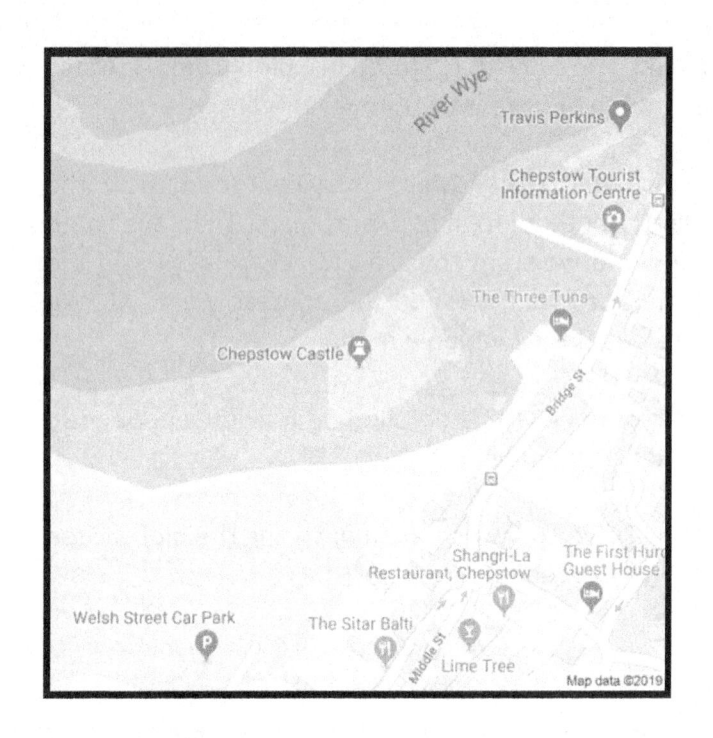

You can make far more complex maps. Check out the Maps service here:
https://developers.google.com/apps-script/reference/maps/maps

7 – Getting contents of a Drive folder

So far, we've been creating files and folders in our Drive, but it's also useful to find out what's already on there to then work with certain files or folders.

In this chapter we'll look at:

- Logging the name of every folder on the user's Drive
- Logging the name of every folder in a particular folder
- Getting the folders in a folder and changing all the names
- Finding a particular folder by its name and adding a newly-created file in there
- Logging the name of all the files in a particular folder

Example 71 – Logging the name of every folder on the user's Drive

In this first example, we're going to get every folder that's stored on My Drive. Depending on how folders you have, this can take a while to run. Then, it will log the folder names in the log.

```
1. // Log the name of every folder in the user's Drive
2. function example71() {
3.   const folders = DriveApp.getFolders();
4.   while (folders.hasNext()) {
5.     var folder = folders.next();
6.     Logger.log(folder.getName());
7.   }
8. }
```

L2: Set up the function.

L3: First, we get the folders in the Drive, using the **getFolders()** method on **DriveApp**, then store the content in the variable *folders*.

L4: Now, to access that information and to create a list of the folders, we need to loop through it. As we don't know before had how many folders we have, we can't use a **for** loop, but instead we can use a **while** loop. This will continue looping while there is content.

The **while** loop structure is this:

While (condition) {
  Do something
}

We start with the **while** keyword and then in the brackets we use the **hasNext()** method on the variable *folders*. So, as it gets the folders one by one, if there is another folder left in the *folders* content, the loop will continue.

L5: Here we will get that next folder, using the **next()** method and store it in the variable *folder*.

L6: It gets the name of the folder and logs it.

L7: Close the loop.

L8: Close the function.

As you can see, it's listed the folders on my Drive (at least this is a snapshot of them). Note, they are not in alphabetical order.

Execution log

9:56:40 PM	Notice	Execution started
9:56:42 PM	Info	EXAMPLE41-FOLDER1
9:56:42 PM	Info	EXAMPLE41-FOLDER2
9:56:42 PM	Info	EXAMPLE 24 SUB FOLDER

Example 72 – Getting the folder names within a specific folder

We can also find out the folders in a particular folder. The code is similar but first we'll have to get the folder we want to investigate.

```
10.  //Get folder names within a specific folder
11.  function example72() {
12.    const parentFolder =
    DriveApp.getFolderById('14g-
    tlUGinVlMxA77VUZu6TKi5-zXcDdJ');
13.    const folders =
    parentFolder.getFolders();
14.    while (folders.hasNext()) {
15.      var folder = folders.next();
16.      Logger.log(folder.getName());
17.    }
18.  }
```

L11: Set up the function.

75

L12: Get the folder by its ID and store it in the variable *parentFolder*. Note, I've shortened the folder and file IDs in this chapter, so the code is easier to read.

L13: Get the folders in the *parentFolder* and store it in variable *folders*.

L14: Use the while loop to get all the folders in that folder and store them in *folders*.

L15: Here we will get that next folder, using the **next()** method and store it in the variable *folder*.

L16: Get the name of the folder and log it.

L17: Close the loop.

L18: Close the function.

Here are all the folders in that folder:

9:57:05 PM	Info	EXAMPLE41-FOLDER2
9:57:05 PM	Info	EXAMPLE 24 SUB FOLDER
9:57:05 PM	Info	FOLDER 10
9:57:05 PM	Info	FOLDER 9

Example 73 – Changing all the folder names in a specific folder

Being able to access all the folders in a folder, means we can work on them one by one. Here we'll get the folders in a folder, then rename them all with "FOLDER " and a consecutive number.

```
20.  //Change all folder names within a specific
     folder
21.  function example73() {
22.    const parentFolder =
       DriveApp.getFolderById('14g-
       tlUGinVlMxA77VUZu6TKi5-zXcDdJ');
23.    const folders =
       parentFolder.getFolders();
24.    var n = 0;
25.    while (folders.hasNext()) {
26.      var folder = folders.next();
27.      n++;
28.      folder.setName("FOLDER "+n);
29.    }
30.  }
```

L21: Set up the function.

L22: Get the folder by its ID and store it in *parentFolder*.

L23: Get the folders in that folder and store them in *folders*.

L24: As we want to add consecutive numbers, we need to set up a counter. We'll use the variable *n* to keep count and start it at 0.

L25: We use the while loop to loop through our folders.

L26: We get each folder and store it *folder*.

L27: Let's increase the counter *n* by 1, using ++ to add 1 to it.

L28: Let's set the name of the folder to "FOLDER " and add the number stored in n.

L29: Close the loop.

L30: Close the function.

As you can see it's renamed all the folders:

📁   FOLDER 1

📁   FOLDER 2

📁   FOLDER 3

Example 74 – Getting a folder by its name, making a copy of a file and adding it in the folder

Here we're going to search for a folder by its name in a specific folder and then make a copy of a document and place it in that folder. This is mainly to show you how you can get the list of folders and then pick out certain ones that meet a particular criterion.

```
32.  //Get specific folder by name, get its ID
33.  //make a copy of a file and add it in that
     folder
34.  function example74() {
35.    const parentFolder =
       DriveApp.getFolderById('14g-
       tlUGinVlMxA77VUZu6TKi5-zXcDdJ');
36.    const folders =
       parentFolder.getFolders();
```

```
37.      while (folders.hasNext()) {
38.        var folder = folders.next();
39.        if(folder.getName() === "FOLDER 3"){
40.          var folderId = folder.getId();
41.          var folder3 =
   DriveApp.getFolderById(folderId);
42.          const masterFile =
   DriveApp.getFileById('15UR9rxKfHcJb0Ws7VaIFG
   gJ2eqov2o50wJY7nm2fnR8');
43.          masterFile.makeCopy("New Doc",
   folder3);
44.        }
45.      }
46.    }
```

L34: Set up the function.

L35: Get the folder by its ID.

L36: Get the folders in that folder.

L37: Loop through the folders.

L38: Get the next folder.

L39: Here we're going to use a conditional statement to see if the name of the folder matches "FOLDER 3". If it does it will run the code in between the curly brackets.

The structure of an **if** statement is:

if (condition to check) {
  If it's true, run the code here. If not, ignore it.
}

79

We get the folder's name and then check if it's the same (note the 3 equals signs) as "FOLDER 3". Then open the curly brackets.

If the name is FOLDER 3, then we run lines 40 to 43.

L40: Get the folder's ID.

L41: Get the folder by its ID and store it in the variable *folder3*.

L42: Get the master file by its ID and store it in the variable *masterFile*.

L43: Make a copy of that file and place it in the FOLDER 3 folder.

L44: Close the **if** statement.

L45: Close the while loop.

L46: Close the function.

If we look in FOLDER 3, we can see it's placed the newly-created document in there.

📁   FOLDER 3
📄   New Doc

Example 75 – Getting filenames in a folder

We can't just get folders, we can also get all the files in a folder too.

```
48.  //Get file names in a folder
49.  function example75() {
50.    const parentFolder = 
   DriveApp.getFolderById('14g-
   tlUGinVlMxA77VUZu6TKi5-zXcDdJ');
51.    const files = parentFolder.getFiles();
52.    while (files.hasNext()) {
53.      var file = files.next();
54.      Logger.log(file.getName());
55.    }
56.  }
```

L49: Set up the function.

L50: Get the folder by its ID.

L51: This time we get the files in that folder using the **getFiles()** method and store it in the variable *files*.

L52: We loop through the files.

L53: We add the next file to the variable *file*.

L54: Then log the name of the file in the log.

L55-56: Close the loop and the function.

As we can see, it's logged all the files in that folder.

```
9:59:11 PM    Info      EXAMPLE 61 - Company document.pdf
9:59:11 PM    Info      Master document
9:59:11 PM    Info      NEW SHORTCUT-To File 'Weekly Presentation'
```

8 – Getting files by type

There are times where we want to get certain types of files and then edit them, for example, get all the Google Docs in a folder then add some text.

In this chapter, we're going to look at:
- Getting all the Google Docs in a folder and then adding a piece of text in all of them
- Deleting all Google Sheets in a folder that haven't been updated for over a week

Example 81 – Getting any Google Docs in a folder and adding a paragraph in all of them

Here we're going to get all the Google Docs in a specific folder, then add a paragraph to all of them. It's great to get files in this way, as it much quicker than getting all the files in a folder, then filtering by a particular type. You'll see how quick and easy it is to update documents.

```
1.  //Get any Google Docs in folder and add a
    paragraph to all of them
2.  function example81() {
3.    const parentFolder =
    DriveApp.getFolderById('14g-
    tlUGinVlMxA77VUZu6TKi5-zXcDdJ');
4.    const listOfDocs =
    parentFolder.getFilesByType(MimeType.GOOGLE_
    DOCS);
5.    while (listOfDocs.hasNext()) {
6.      var file = listOfDocs.next();
7.      var docId = file.getId();
8.      var doc = DocumentApp.openById(docId);
9.      var body = doc.getBody();
```

```
10.         body.appendParagraph("This paragraph 
    was added automatically.");
11.     }
12. }
```

L2: Set up the function.

L3: Get the folder by its ID.

L4: Get the files of a particular type by using the **getFilesbyType()** method. In the brackets, state the type you're looking for, in this case they are Google Docs. Store them in the variable *listOfDocs*.

L5: Now loop through that list using **while**.

L6: Get the next file and store it in the variable *file*.

To be able to add a paragraph to a document, we need get its ID, open it by that ID, then get its body and finally, append the paragraph to that body.

L7: Get the file's ID and store it in *docId*.

L8: Open the document by this ID, using **DocumentApp** and the **openById()** method, similar to what we used to open a spreadsheet in an earlier chapter. Store this in the variable *doc*.

L9: Get the body of the document by using **getBody()** and store it in the variable *body*.

L10: Get that document body and append a paragraph to it using **appendParagraph()**. Add the text you want to add in

83

between the brackets. This will add the text to the bottom of the document.

L11: Close the loop.

L12: Close the function.

Run the script and we'll see that it's append the paragraph at the bottom of the documents, after the table.

Name:	
Company:	
Coordinator:	

This paragraph was added automatically.

Example 82 – Deleting all the files of a specific type that haven't been updated for over a week

Apps Script can also help you with a bit of Drive housekeeping. We may want to delete any files that haven't been updated for a period of time from a folder. Rather than search for these manually and delete them one-by-one we can get a script to do the job.

Here we're going to search for and delete any Google Sheets that haven't been updated for over a week.

IMPORTANT - Obviously when it comes to deleting files, make sure you've set it up so it doesn't delete something you want to keep! The good thing is that these aren't really deleted, they are moved to the trash/bin, so you could recover them if you've deleted something by mistake.

```
14.  //Delete files of a specific type that
     haven't been updated for over a week
15.  function example82() {
16.    const parentFolder =
       DriveApp.getFolderById('1bG6AKxsFl_H-
       vx903vp4Kyw0yqvE3V-1');
17.    const listOfSsheets =
       parentFolder.getFilesByType(MimeType.GOOGLE_
       SHEETS);
18.    while (listOfSsheets.hasNext()) {
19.      var file = listOfSsheets.next();
20.      if (new Date() - file.getLastUpdated()
       > 7 * 24 * 60 * 60 * 1000) {
21.        file.setTrashed(true);
22.      }
23.    }
24.  }
```

L15: Set up the function.

L16: Get the folder by its ID.

L17: This time we're getting any Google Sheets in that folder and we'll store them in the variable *listOfSsheets*.

L18: Loop through the spreadsheets found.

L19: Every time around the loop, store the next spreadsheet in the variable *file*.

L20: Now we want to check if the file hasn't been updated for more than a week. First, we need to set up an **if** statement and

85

the condition we add will get today's date, subtract when the file was last updated from it and then check to see if that more than a week ago.

To get today's date we use: **new Date()**. This returns a date and time in milliseconds.

To get when the file was last updated we use the **getLastUpdated()** method on the file.

Subtracting that from today's date will leave us with a difference in milliseconds.

A week in milliseconds is 7 (days) x 24 (hours) x 60 (mins) x 60 (seconds) x 1000 (milliseconds). You can of course adjust this to your needs.

So we check to see if the difference is more than a week, if it is we run the code in line 21, if not we ignore it.

L21: If it's more than a week, we delete the file by using the **setTrashed()** method and state *true*.

L22: Close the if statement.

L23: Close the loop.

L24: Close the function.

In the folder I had these 2 files and they are now in the bin/trash:

📄 3-folder URL

📄 Drive & Docs Plan

We could adapt this code to make a useful archiver, where it could move files not updated for a period of time, to an archive folder.

9 – Creating download URLs

Files from Drive can be downloaded by editing their URLs, which is also great for sharing. For example, you may have a document on your Drive which you want to allow people to download as a PDF, without having to store that document as a PDF on your Drive, using your Drive space and not allowing you to be able to update the document easily.

We're going to look at two ways to create download links. Also we're going to work with multiple functions, which allows us to use pieces of code with different functions, without having to duplicate them. It also keeps the different parts of the script clearly separate so it could be easier to understand and to correct any problems.

In this chapter, we'll look at:

- Creating a download link for a PDF created from a Google Doc and then emailing it
- Getting a file by its name
- Using the built-in **getdownloadUrl()** method
- Getting a file, creating a PDF from it and storing it in a folder, then emailing the link to it

Example 91 – Creating a PDF download link and emailing it

Here we're going to get a document called "Reference Doc", create a PDF download link for it and email that link, allowing the email recipient to download the PDF from the link in the email.

We're also going to call two separate functions. One to get the file ID, and the other to send the email.

```
1.  //Get file 'Reference Doc', make PDF
    download link & email it
2.  function example91() {
3.    var fileId = getFileId();
4.
5.    var downloadUrl =
    'https://docs.google.com/document/d/'
6.      + fileId + '/export?format=pdf';
7.
8.    sendEmail(downloadUrl);
9.  }
```

L2: Set up function *example91*.

L3: What's happening here is that the *getFileId()* function is called and the code in it is run, which will find a file called "Reference Doc" and then return its file ID. That ID is then stored in the variable *fileId*.

I'll go through how that function works a little later.

L5-6: Now we create the download URL from that file ID.

The structure of the URL to convert a Google Doc into a PDF download link is this (all joined together in as one URL):

https://docs.google.com/document/d/
FILE ID
/export?format=pdf

89

So, we state the fixed parts at the start and end of the URL and add the file ID in the middle. We then store what we've create in the variable *downloadUrl*.

L8: We then call the *sendEmail* function to send the email, and in the brackets we send the download URL to that function. We don't need a variable here as this function doesn't return anything.

L9: Close the function.

Now, we need to create two functions, one for getting the file ID, *getFileId()*, and the other to send the email, *sendEmail()*.

Rather than putting these functions on the same page, let's create a separate script file, to keep them separate and to keep the scripts on each file shorter.

Click on the plus icon next to "Files".

Files   +

Then select "Script".

+ ↶

Script

Let's call this file "commonFunctions".

Files	+
examples.gs	⋮
commonFunctions	

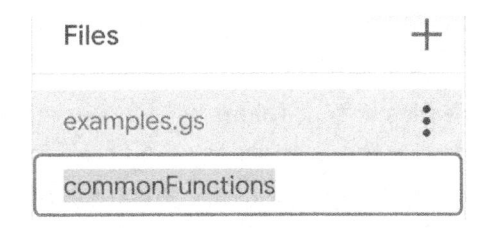

Note, I've renamed the original script file from "Code" to "examples". Click on the 3 dots to rename a file.

Let's look at the first function that we call in the *example91* function above, "getFileId". The code is going to be similar to what we saw in the last chapter.

```
1. //Gets files named "Reference Doc" and
   return file ID
2. function getFileId() {
3.   const folder =
     DriveApp.getFolderById('14g-
     tlUGinVlMxA77VUZu6TKi5-zXcDdJ');
4.   var files =
     folder.getFilesByName('Reference Doc');
5.   while (files.hasNext()) {
6.     var file = files.next();
7.     var fileId = file.getId();
8.     return fileId;
9.   }
10. }
```

L2: Set up the function *getFileId*.

L3: Get the folder where the file we're looking for is in by its ID.

L4: We want to get the file called "Reference Doc" in that folder, Using the **getFilesByName()** method means I can get the file without having to know its ID initially. Store that in the *files* variable.

Note, that if there were more files in that folder by that name, this code won't find the others, as the loop stops when the file ID is returned, but it stops at the first one it finds, which might not necessarily by the one you want.

L5: Loop through the *files* variable.

L6: Get the next file in *files*.

L7: Get the file ID and store it in *fileId*. This is what we need to create the download URL.

L8: Return the file ID to the original function. This is what is picked up in line 3 of the *example91* function.

L9: Close the loop.

L10: Close the function.

We also need a function to send the email. In the same script file as the *getFileId* function, write the following function.

```
12.    //Send email with download link
13.    function sendEmail(downloadUrl) {
14.
       MailApp.sendEmail('bazrobertsbooks@gmail.com',
15.        'Reference Doc - Download Link',
16.        'Download the file from here: '
17.        + downloadUrl);
18.    }
```

L13: Set up the function *sendEmail*. We need the download URL from the *example91* function, so we add the *downloadUrl* variable in the brackets.

L14-16: To send the email we use the **MailApp** service and use the **sendEmail()** method. There different versions of this method and here we're going to use the one which needs 3 parameters in the brackets: email address(es), email title, email message.

To send the download link, add the text and then add the *downloadUrl* variable.

L18: Close the function.

OK, that's probably a lot to take in, as we are working with 3 different functions. So, let me just summarize the main steps of what's happening:

1-Run function *example91*
2-It runs function *getFileId*, this gets the file called "Reference Doc" and returns the ID of the document.
3-Function example91 receives this ID and stores it in the variable *fileId*.
4-It creates the download URL using the file ID.
5-It calls the *sendEmail* function and sends the *downloadUrl* variable to it.
6-Function *sendEmail* receives the download URL and sends the email with the link in it.

The recipient will receive an email like this:

93

baz@bazroberts.com
to me

Download the file from here:
https://docs.google.com/document/d/1KXkWUGkfw5Z-pQJX77yrdVGQaPcPgWq2LGm0YOUbWaA/export?format=pdf

Reference doc

Clicking on the link will download the file as a PDF (even though in the email it appears as a Google Doc).

Underneath the link the recipient will also have the option to add a shortcut to that file to their Drive.

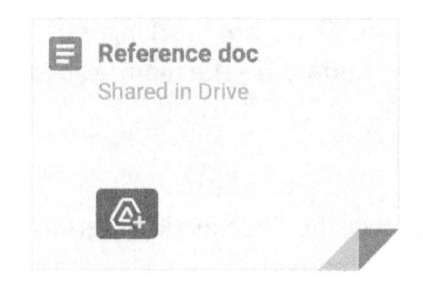

Reference doc
Shared in Drive

Note, we could change it so that a Microsoft Word compatible document is downloaded instead. All we would need to do is change the last part from *pdf* to *doc*.

https://docs.google.com/document/d/FILE ID/export?format=**doc**

Example 92 – Getting a file by name, creating a PDF of it and storing it in a specific folder

In this example, we're going to get the file as before, but this time we're going to make PDF of it on our Drive and then log the download URL. We could easily email the URLs as before, but let's see what link is produced this time.

This time we have 4 functions, *example92*, *getFileInfo*, *makePdf*, and *sendEmail*.

```
11.  //Get file 'Reference Doc', make PDF, add
       to folder,
12.  //get download URL and email it
13.  function example92() {
14.    var fileInfo = getFileInfo();
15.
16.    var docPdf = makePdf(fileInfo);
17.
18.    var downloadUrl =
       docPdf.getDownloadUrl();
19.
20.    docPdf.addViewer('brgablog@gmail.com');
21.
22.    sendEmail(downloadUrl);
23.  }
```

L13: Set up function *example92*.

L14: Call function *getFileInfo* and store the returned data in the variable *fileInfo*.

L16: Call function *makePdf* and pass the *fileInfo* variable. Store the returned document (the PDF) in the variable *docPdf*.

L18: Rather than creating a download URL manually, let's use the built-in **getDownloadUrl()** method.

The issue I find with the **getDownloadUrl()** method is that you can run into permission issues. If the recipient doesn't have access to the file or folder you're using, or if it's not open to anyone with a link, then they won't be able to download it. They will see this message when clicking on the link:

Google

403. That's an error.

We're sorry, but you do not have access to this page.
That's all we know.

L20: To get around that, you may need to add this line to add the recipient as a viewer of the file, allowing them to download it.

L22: Call the *sendEmail* function and pass the *downloadUrl* variable.

L23: Close the function.

Now let's look at the *getFileInfo* function. We write this in the *commonFunctions* script file.

This will get the folder and get any files called "Reference Doc". It will then return the file, with three pieces of information: file ID, the file, the folder.

```
20.  //Gets files named "Reference Doc" and
     return file ID
21.  function getFileInfo() {
22.      const folder = DriveApp.getFolderById('14g-tlUGinVlMxA77VUZu6TKi5-zXcDdJ');
23.      var files = folder.getFilesByName('Reference Doc');
24.      while (files.hasNext()) {
25.          var file = files.next();
26.          var fileId = file.getId();
27.
28.          return {
29.              fileId: fileId,
30.              file: file,
31.              folder: folder
32.          }
33.      }
34.  }
```

L21: Set up function *getFileInfo*.

L22: Get the folder by its ID.

L23: Get any files called "Reference Doc".

L24: Loop through the files.

L25: Get the next file in *files*.

L26: Get its ID.

L28-32: Here, as we want to return multiple pieces of information, we're going to set up some **properties**. We wrap all these properties in a set of curly brackets. Then each

97

property has a name and a value linked together with a colon, i.e. Property name : value
When there is more than one, we link them together with commas, similar to what we do in arrays.

Here's what is returned:

```
{folder=Example Folder (Don't delete), file=Reference doc, fileId=17aBdjsbMAdJ4jsEufMyaD8YR9Xq9uM4AQNog_MZd9LU}
```

You can see the information is stored in property=value pairs, wrapped up in curly brackets. This allows us to return it all in one go and to be stored in one variable. Later on we can easily extract the pieces of information we need.

L33: Close the loop.

L34: Close the function.

The third function is what makes the PDF and adds it to our folder.

```
36.   //Get file by ID, make PDF, add PDF to folder
37.   function makePdf(fileInfo) {
38.     const pdf = DriveApp.getFileById(fileInfo.fileId)
39.       .getAs('application/pdf');
40.     pdf.setName(fileInfo.file.getName() + ".pdf");
41.
42.     const docPdf = DriveApp.createFile(pdf);
43.     docPdf.moveTo(fileInfo.folder);
44.     return docPdf;
45.   }
```

L37: Set up function *makePdf* and receives the *fileInfo* variable sent from the *example92* function.

L38: Get the file by its ID. In the brackets, we extract the file ID from the *fileInfo* variable by using a dot and the name of the property we returned from the *getFileInfo* function.

Object.property > fileInfo.fileId

L39: We then get the file as a PDF, then store it in the variable *pdf*.

L40: Set the PDF name using the name of the document stored in *file* property and adding the file extension .pdf. (Object.property.method())

L42: Create the PDF from the *pdf* blob and store it in *docPdf*.

L43: This will have created a PDF in our My Drive, so we need to move it to the folder we want, using **moveTo()**. Then pass the *folder* property in the brackets.

L44: Then return the PDF in the variable *docPdf*.

L45: Close the function.

So, again let's just summarize what's happening.

1-Run function *example92*, this calls function *getFileInfo*.
2-This gets the folder, gets the document in the folder by name, and its ID, and returns all 3 pieces of data as properties (fileId, file, folder).

99

3-This is received by the *example92* function and stored in the fileInfo variable.
4-Calls function *makePdf* and passes over the *fileInfo* variable.
5-Function *makePdf* makes the PDF using the 3 properties and moves it to the folder we want.
6-Gets the download URL from PDF document returned.
7-Adds the recipient as a viewer to the file.
8-Sends an email containing the download URL.

Run the *example92* function and we'll see it's sent an email with a link to download the PDF.

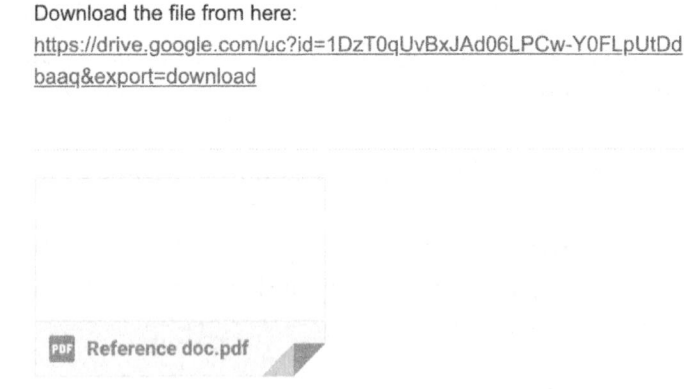

Download the file from here:
https://drive.google.com/uc?id=1DzT0qUvBxJAd06LPCw-Y0FLpUtDdbaaq&export=download

📄 Reference doc.pdf

The benefit of this method is that when you hover over the PDF at the bottom of the email, it gives you the opportunity of either downloading or storing the PDF on your Drive.

Note, as we are also sharing the file with the recipient, they will receive an automated email telling them it's shared.

10 – Automatically send a brochure when a form is submitted

The chapters so far have needed us to run the scripts. In this chapter, we're going to see how we can automate this with the use of a trigger.

As an example, we're going to create a form which will ask the user to fill in their email address to request a brochure. When the form is submitted, this will trigger the script, which will get our brochure, which has been made in Google Slides, convert it into a PDF, then email it to the prospective client.

Example 101 – Automatically sending a brochure when a form is submitted

Create the brochure
Here, I've created a simple brochure using Google Slides.

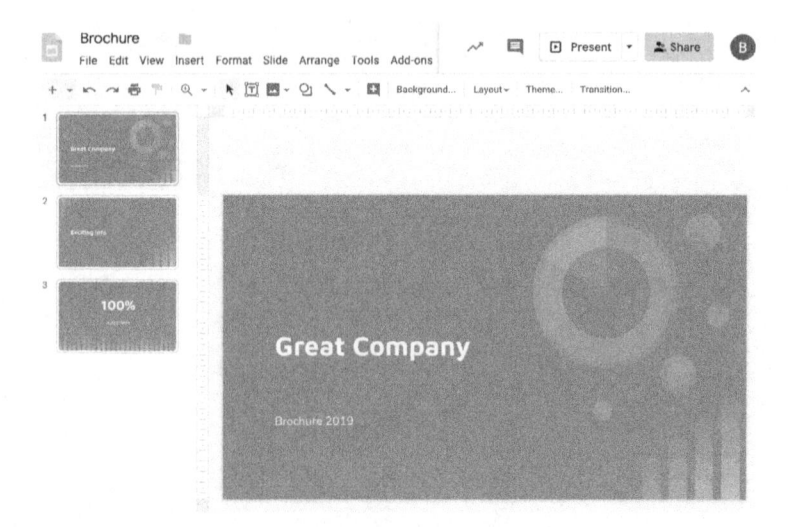

Create and set up the form

Here we're going to write a quick little script to create a form that will request an email address from the form-filler. Write this in a standalone script as we have been doing so far in this book.

```
1. function createForm() {
2.   const form = FormApp.create("Brochure request");
3.   form.setTitle('Brochure request');
4.   form.setCollectEmail(true);
5. }
```

L1: Set up the function.

L2: Create a new form using the **FormApp** and the **create()** method and name it.

L3: Get the form and set the title. This is the title the user sees.

L4: All the form will have is a question asking for the user's email address. We do that by using **setCollectEmail()** and setting it to true. This is the equivalent of going to the form's settings menu and ticking the "Collect email addresses" option.

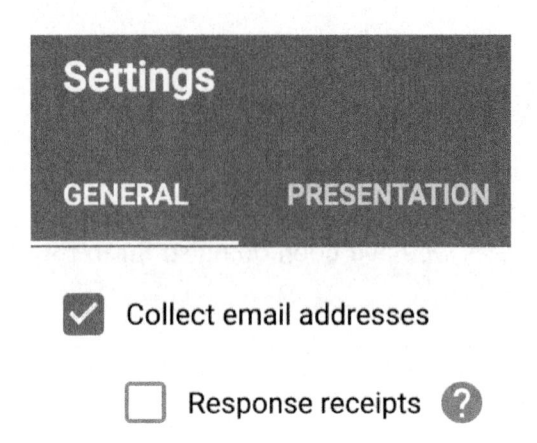

Settings

GENERAL   PRESENTATION

☑ Collect email addresses

☐ Response receipts ❓

Line 5: Close the function.

Run the script and this will create a new form in our My Drive. You may need to move it to another folder.

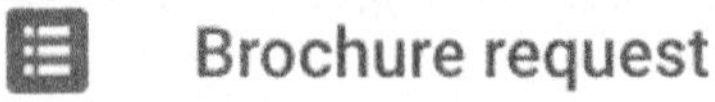

▤   **Brochure request**

As you can see it's set it up the way we want it.

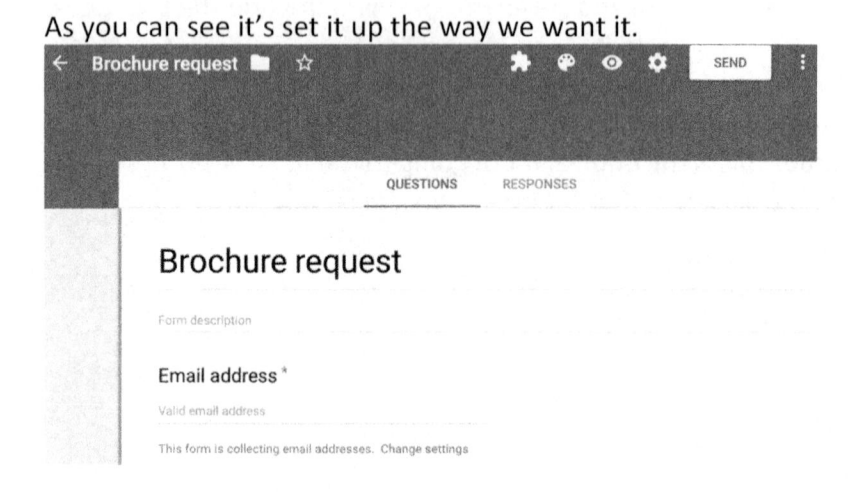

← Brochure request 📁 ☆   ✱ 🎨 👁 ⚙ [SEND]

QUESTIONS   RESPONSES

Brochure request

Form description

Email address *

Valid email address

This form is collecting email addresses. Change settings

The user sees this:

Brochure request

*Required

Email address *

Your email address

⬜ Send me a copy of my responses.

SUBMIT

You can delete the "Send me a copy of my responses" option by going to the settings cog and unticking the response receipts option.

<u>Opening the script Editor within the Form</u>

All the examples so far in this book have run as standalone scripts but this time we're going to write the script within this form, so it is "bound" to this form, i.e. it runs from within it. This means that the script lives within the form and you need to open the form to access it.

This is important as we're going to set up the trigger to this form and that's what will run the script automatically.

To access the Script Editor, open the form and click on the 3-dots menu at the top of the screen and click "Script Editor" from the menu.

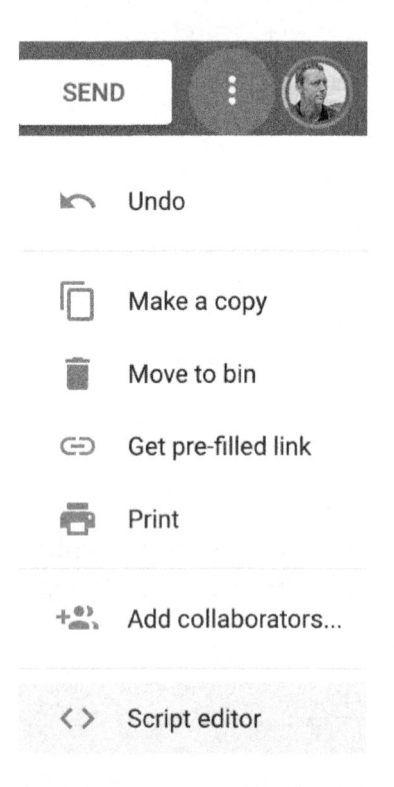

- Undo
- Make a copy
- Move to bin
- Get pre-filled link
- Print
- Add collaborators...
- Script editor

This will open the Script Editor.

The form script

Now let's look at the script. In summary this will:

106

1) Get the latest form response and extract the client's email address from it.
2) Get the Slides presentation and convert it into a PDF.
3) Send an email to the client with the PDF attached.

```
1. //Send brochure PDF when form filled out
2. function example101() {
3.   //Get email
4.   const form = FormApp.getActiveForm();
5.   const responses = form.getResponses();
6.   const latestResponse = responses[responses.length-1];
7.   const emailAddress = latestResponse.getRespondentEmail();
```

L2: Set up the function.

L4: Get the active form, which is this one, and store it in the *form* variable.

L5: Get all the form responses in *form* and store them in *responses*. This is an array of responses.

L6: Get the latest response by getting the last response in the *responses* array. We do that by getting the length of the array and subtracting 1, as arrays are zero-based. I.e. the first response is in position 0, the second in position 1, and so on.

L7: This last response will contain their email address. We get that by using the **getRespondentEmail()** method. We then store that in *emailAddress*.

To learn more about using scripts with Forms, check out my Apps Script book "Beginner's Guide to Apps Script 2 – Forms".

Now we know who to send the email to. Next, is to make the PDF.

```
9.      //Get Slides and create PDF
10.       const brochure =
        DriveApp.getFileById('1vF-
        Q7_OA6rhbI8DvAcuMvpkrm3iPb7Ua9eqDjuBbq7w')
11.
          .getAs(MimeType.PDF);
```

L10-11: We get the Slides brochure file by its ID and then get it as a PDF. We then store that in the variable *brochure*.

The final part is to email the brochure.

```
13.       //Send PDF in email
14.       MailApp.sendEmail(emailAddress,
15.                         'BROCHURE',
16.                         'Please find attached
        this year\'s brochure.',
17.                         {attachments: brochure,
18.                          name: 'Brochure
        2021'})
19.     }
```

L14: We use the **MailApp** and the **sendEmail()** method to send the email. There are 3 main parameters. The first is who we are sending the email to. Here we use the *emailAddress* variable.

L15: We then state the email title, "BROCHURE".

L16: We add the message we want in the email. Note, the forward slash in *year's*. This is so it treats the apostrophe before the *s* as text and not the end of the text string.

L17: As we are also going to include an attachment, we need to add a couple options. The first is the attachment, we use curly brackets for the options, and then add "attachments:" and the *brochure* variable, followed by a comma.

L18: Then we add "name:" and the name of the brochure PDF we want the user to see. Close the curly brackets and the normal ones.

L19: Close the function.

Setting up the trigger

The final step is to set up the trigger so that this runs automatically. We can write a little script to build this for us.

```
21.   function setUpTrigger() {
22.       var form = FormApp.getActiveForm();
23.       ScriptApp.newTrigger('example101')
24.       .forForm(form)
25.       .onFormSubmit()
26.       .create();
27.   }
```

L21: Set up the function *setUpTrigger*.

L22: Get the active form and store it in *form*.

L23: We use the **ScriptApp** to set up triggers. We will chain 4 methods together. First, we add the **newTrigger()** method and state which function it will run, when triggered. So, here we put the name of the function we've just written.

L24: It's on a form, so we add the **forForm()** method and pass the *form* variable.

L25: We state the type of trigger, in this case it runs when a form is submitted, so type in the **onFormSubmit()** method.

L26: Finally, we need to create it, using you've guessed it, the **create()** method.

L27: Close the function.

Run the script. Note, you may have to authorize the script again during that process, as it's added an extra service, **ScriptApp**.

If you click on the Triggers icon on the toolbar, you will see it's added the trigger.

⏰ Triggers

Triggers

+ Add a filter

Owned by	Last run	Deployment	Event	Function
Me	-	Head	From form - On form submit	example101

Sometimes it's just quicker to set up the trigger manually.

Setting up the trigger manually

Click on the Triggers icon.

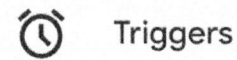

⏰ Triggers

This will open the triggers page. Click on "+ Add Trigger"-

[+ Add Trigger]

This is where you configure the trigger. As we only have one function, this is very simple to do and the only thing we need to change is the trigger type.

Under "Select event type", choose "On form submit". This is the type of trigger. It means that it will be run when the form is submitted.

Add Trigger for 10-send PDF

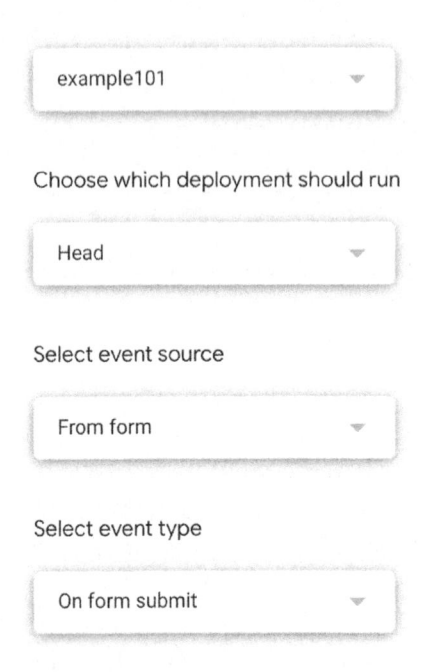

[example101 ▾]

Choose which deployment should run

[Head ▾]

Select event source

[From form ▾]

Select event type

[On form submit ▾]

Then click Save.

Cancel   **Save**

This will create the trigger.

Owned by	Last run	Deployment	Event	Function
Me	-	Head	From form - On form submit	example101

It's useful to know this process in case you want to delete or edit any triggers, which can be done from this same page.

It's now all ready. The potential clients fill in the form and they automatically receive this email:

Brochure 2021
to me ▼

Please find attached this year's brochure.

11 – Searching files & folders

DriveApp has the ability to search your files and folders using certain search terms. Here we'll look at:

- Searching for files with a single search term
- Searching for files with multiple search terms
- Searching for folders and listing the results in a Google Doc

Example 111 – Searching for files that meet search criteria

Here we're going to get a list of all the files in a specific folder that have been modified since the end of March 2021.

```
1. //search for files
2. function example111() {
3.   const files =
     DriveApp.getFolderById('1bG6AKxsFl_H-vx903vp4Kyw0yqvE3V-1')
4.     .searchFiles('modifiedDate > "2021-03-31"');
5.   while (files.hasNext()) {
6.     var file = files.next();
7.     Logger.log(file.getName());
8.   }
9. }
```

L2: Set up function.

L3: Get the folder by its ID. Don't add a semi-colon on the end as we're going to chain the next method to it.

L4: Add the **searchFiles()** method. In the brackets you need to add the search term. We add the **modifiedDate** term and any dates greater than 31st Mar 21. This will list of the files that match those criteria. Store them in *files*.

L5: Now, we need to loop through the *files* variable using the while loop.

L6: We get the next file and store it in the variable *file*.

L7: Log the name of the file.

L8: Close the loop.

L9: Close the function.

Run the script and we will see the list of files in that folder which have been modified since March.

Execution log

2:52:00 PM	Notice	Execution started
2:52:01 PM	Info	11-search files and folders
2:52:01 PM	Info	10-Send brochure
2:52:01 PM	Info	9-downloadUrl
2:52:01 PM	Info	8-Get files by type

Example 112 – Searching for files that meet multiple search criteria

Here we're going to do the same thing, except we only want to see files modified since March that contain the word 'folders' in them.

```
11.    //search for files - multiple search terms
12.    function example112() {
13.      const files =
       DriveApp.getFolderById('1bG6AKxsFl_H-
       vx903vp4Kyw0yqvE3V-1')
14.      .searchFiles('modifiedDate > "2021-03-01"
       and title contains "folders"');
15.      while (files.hasNext()) {
16.        var file = files.next();
17.        Logger.log(file.getName());
18.      }
19.    }
```

L12-13: Same as above.

L14: The **searchFiles()** method con contain multiple search terms by connecting them with the keyword **and**. Note, modified date and titles are used here. Be careful with the single and double quote marks here.

L15-19: As above.

As we can see it's filtered the previous list by only including those filenames with the word "folders" in them.

2:53:52 PM	Info	11-search files and folders
2:53:52 PM	Info	4-Add & remove files and folders
2:53:52 PM	Info	3-make Copies of Files and Folders
2:53:52 PM	Info	2-Creating files & folders in specific folders
2:53:52 PM	Info	1-Creating files and folders in My Drive

Example 113 – Searching for folders and listing the result in a Google Doc

We can also search for folders within folders and instead of just logging the folder names we can list them in a Google Doc.

```
21. //search for folders
22. function example113() {
23.    const doc = DocumentApp.create("Folders list");
24.    const folders = DriveApp.getFolderById('14g-tlUGinVlMxA77VUZu6TKi5-zXcDdJ')
25.       .searchFolders('title contains "folder"');
26.    while (folders.hasNext()) {
27.       var folder = folders.next();
28.       Logger.log(folder.getName());
29.       doc.getBody().appendParagraph(folder.getName());
30.    }
31. }
```

L22: Set up function.

L23: Create a new Google Doc ready to be populated and store it in *doc*.

117

L24-25: Get all the folders in the folder, which contain "folder" in the folder name.

L26: Loop through the folders.

L27: Get each folder and store it in folder.

L28: Log the name of the folder.

L29: Get the document in *doc*, get its body and append a paragraph with the folder's name.

L30-31: Close the loop and function.

Run the script and we will see it's found 2 folders with the word "folder" in them.

In our My Drive, we can see it's created a Google Doc called Folders List.

📄　　Folders list

Opening the Google Doc we can see it's added the list of folders in there.

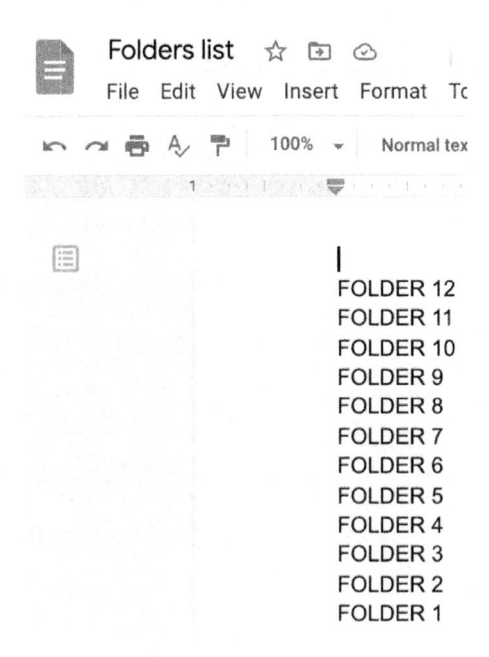

```
Folders list
File  Edit  View  Insert  Format  Tc

             |
             FOLDER 12
             FOLDER 11
             FOLDER 10
             FOLDER 9
             FOLDER 8
             FOLDER 7
             FOLDER 6
             FOLDER 5
             FOLDER 4
             FOLDER 3
             FOLDER 2
             FOLDER 1
```

You can find more information on the search criteria here: https://developers.google.com/apps-script/reference/drive/drive-app#searchFiles(String)

https://developers.google.com/drive/api/v3/search-shareddrives

Now, you should have a good understanding of how to use the Drive service and how you can use it with other services too.

Appendix 1 - Links to the complete scripts

Below are links to the scripts in all the chapters, where you can copy and paste them and use them in your projects. All are stored on GitHub.

Chapter 1
http://bit.ly/2JCrLLL

Chapter 2
http://bit.ly/2XHrfGw

Chapter 3
http://bit.ly/2G7OYoh

Chapter 4
http://bit.ly/2G5eA5l

Chapter 5
http://bit.ly/2XCHVyz

Chapter 6
http://bit.ly/2S4apel

Chapter 7
http://bit.ly/2xFgyVl

Chapter 8
http://bit.ly/2LdAoQb

Chapter 9
http://bit.ly/2G2Peow

Chapter 10
http://bit.ly/2NUpVLY

Chapter 11
http://bit.ly/32lVvFA

Appendix 2 – Script Editor tools

Editor
Along the top of the editor, you have the toolbar.

↶ ↷ | 💾 | ▷ Run 🐞 Debug myFunction ▼ | Execution log

Going from left to right we have:

- Undo, redo
- Save (the project)
- Run (the function)
- Debug – Find where there are problems in your code.
- myFunction – This is where you 'll have a list of the functions in that particular script file.
- Execution log – This will open the execution log and show the last program executed with any logs registered.

Helpful Editor tools

The editor is full of tools to make your coding life easier. Below are some of the most useful ones, especially for beginners.

Formatting (indenting) your document

When you type in your code, you should indent sections of the code to make it easier to read. This is not always obvious to a beginner, and even to someone more experienced, manually indenting your code can be time-consuming, so fortunately, there's a shortcut.

Below is code that hasn't been indented:

```
2   function onOpen() {
3   const ss = SpreadsheetApp.getActiveSpreadsheet(),
4   sheet1 = ss.getSheetByName("eg1"),
5   cell = sheet1.getRange("B4");
6   cell.activate()
7   .clearContent();
8   }
```

Right-click somewhere in the code and you'll see a menu. Click on "Format document" (or you can use the keyboard shortcut that is shown.

| Format Document | ⇧⌥F |

This will correctly indent your whole script file. For example, you can see the function is on one level, then the variable on another, and the additional variables, on another.

```
function onOpen() {
  const ss = SpreadsheetApp.getActiveSpreadsheet(),
    sheet1 = ss.getSheetByName("eg1"),
    cell = sheet1.getRange("B4");
  cell.activate()
    .clearContent();
}
```

Highlighting all positions of a variable

When you click on a variable, such as *ss*, it will highlight other instances of that variable, which can help you find where it's being used.

```
const ss = SpreadsheetApp.get
    sheet1 = ss.getSheetByName(
```

Highlighting pairs of brackets

In longer code with multiple brackets, it's sometimes difficult to see the chunk of code contained in a pair of brackets, so it's useful to find the bracket pairs. Plus, it's a way to check the brackets are being paired correctly. Click on one and the paired bracket will be highlighted.

```
function onOpen() {
  const ss = Spreads
    sheet1 = ss.getS
    cell = sheet1.ge
  cell.activate()
    .clearContent();
}
```

Hiding blocks of code

You will notice the downward arrows on the left-hand side of the code. These highlight blocks of code. Sometimes in longer code, it's useful to hide certain ones, to make it easier to concentrate on certain blocks. To hide a block of code, click on the downward arrow next to it.

```
2 ∨ function onOpen() {
3 ∨   const ss = SpreadsheetApp.getActiveS|
4       sheet1 = ss.getSheetByName("eg1"),
5       cell = sheet1.getRange("B4");
6 ∨   cell.activate()
7       .clearContent();
```

As you can see this has hidden lines 4 and 5 which are connected to line 4.

125

```
2 ∨  function onOpen() {
3 >     const ss = Spreads
6 ∨     cell.activate()
7          .clearContent();
```

Find where a variable is defined

You can quickly find where a variable is defined by right-clicking on the variable and selecting Go to definition.

| Go to Definition | ⌘F12 |

This will take you to the line where that variable is defined.

```
const ss = SpreadsheetApp.getActiveSpreadsheet(),
```

Appendix 3 - JavaScript Basics

If you've never used JavaScript before, at first it can look like a foreign language. Which of course in a sense it is, but you'll soon start to see patterns in the code and through the examples you'll see how it all starts connecting together. Apps Script is basically JavaScript with its own special methods. So, a base knowledge of JavaScript is essential if you're going to work with it.

Let's look at some of the fundamental areas that will be used in this book and that are common to most scripts.

Functions

When you open the Script Editor you will see that there is a little bit of code already in there. This is because to run the program you will need to wrap it up in a function giving it an individual name.

```
1    function myFunction() {
2
3    }
```

The function structure is:

Function keyword followed by its name, then followed by a pair of brackets and then a pair of curly brackets.

All the action happens inside the curly brackets. This is where you write your code for that particular function.

Here's a short example. In line 2, I've created a function called example11. On line 3, in between the 2 curly brackets, I put the code that I want to run, when this function is called. In this case, it creates a file on My Drive.

```
//Create a text file
function example11() {
    DriveApp.createFile("EXAMPLE FILE","This is a new file");
}
```

We can have numerous functions in a single script.

Commenting

We can add comments to our code, which is useful to explain what's happening in the code, so it's easier to understand. To create a comment just add 2 backslashes at the start of the line and this will change the colour to light grey. The script will ignore comments.

```
//Create a text file
```

This is also useful to ignore lines of code, maybe temporarily, maybe to check a particular part of a script, or to now run a part whilst you're writing the code.

We can also comment out multiple lines, mainly to ignore a chunk of code. To do so, write a backslash and an asterisk before the code you want to ignore and then an asterisk and a backslash at after it. Here I've commented out lines 13 to 16.

```
function example() {
  /*
      const name = "Barrie Roberts";
      var weather = "Sunny";
  */
  const name = "Fred";
}
```

Service, Class, method

In this book we will be focusing on the Drive service. It's one of many Google Workspace services available and the wonderful thing with Apps Script is that we can write code that use lots of different services together. These are the core Google Workspace services:

G Suite Services
- Calendar
- Contacts
- Data Studio
- Document
- Domain
- Drive
- Forms
- Gmail
- Groups
- Language
- Maps
- Sites
- Slides
- Spreadsheet

In this book, we will also use the Maps, Document, Forms, Slides, and Spreadsheet services.

Within each service we have classes. In the Drive service we have the following classes:

Classes

Name	Brief description
Access	An enum representing classes of users who can access a file or folder, besides any individual users who have been explicitly given access.
DriveApp	Allows scripts to create, find, and modify files and folders in Google Drive.
File	A file in Google Drive.
FileIterator	An iterator that allows scripts to iterate over a potentially large collection of files.
Folder	A folder in Google Drive.
FolderIterator	An object that allows scripts to iterate over a potentially large collection of folders.
Permission	An enum representing the permissions granted to users who can access a file or folder, besides any individual users who have been explicitly given access.
User	A user associated with a file in Google Drive.

Taken from this webpage:
https://developers.google.com/apps-script/reference/drive/

We'll be using the **Access, DriveApp, File, FileIterator, Folder, FolderIterator,** and **Permission** classes, although mainly the **DriveApp, File,** and **Folder** ones.

Drilling down one more level, we have methods. These are the bits of code that do specific jobs and usually have names that are very easy to understand. For example, to create a folder, we use the **createFolder()** method. In this example, we're getting the **DriveApp** class, adding the **createFolder()** method to it and naming that folder "New Folder".

```
DriveApp.createFolder("New folder");
```

Note, in this book, I'll be highlighting classes and methods in **bold**, so they easy to see and find.

= or == or ===
Equals signs can be confusing and are a common mistake. There are 3 types, single, double and triple.

=
The single equals sign <u>assigns</u> a value to a variable. It has nothing to do with something being the same as something else.

In line 2 below, I've assigned 5 to the variable *numb*. So when *numb* is referred to later, it will be referring to 5.

```
function example3() {
  const numb = "5";
  if (numb == 5) {
    Logger.log("1-Number found");
  }

  if (numb === 5) {
    Logger.log("2-Number found");
  }
}
```

131

==

The double equals sign means the 2 values being compared are equal. So, in the example above, line 3 is checking to see if the variable numb is equal to 5.

===

OK, so what's a triple equals sign? This also means the 2 values being compared are equal but it's even stricter. It's not just the value, but things like, is the value type the same?

In our example above, in line 2 I've purposely stored the number as a piece of text and not as a number, which would be without the quote marks. So, when in line 7, it checks to see if *numb* is the same as a number 5, it's checking a piece of text against a number, which isn't the same.

So, the what ends up being logged? Only the first one, as the second check isn't true, so won't run line 8.

```
Info        1-Number found
```

The most common mistake is instead of writing 2 or 3 equals signs to check if something is equal to something you only write one. For example, if(*numb* = 5)... would be incorrect and not do the expected check. The use of the 3 equals signs isn't essential but it can reduce the chance of errors.

Camel case
There is also a style of writing names of variables, functions, etc, called "camel case". This generally is where the words are joined together and the first word is all in lowercase, then the

next words all start with a capital letter. This is to make it easier to read.

```
function thisIsALongFunctionName() {
  var variableUsingCamelCase = 10;
  DriveApp.createFolder("New Folder");
}
```

Here you can see the function name contains 5 words but as there can't be any spaces, it's written as one text string. The variable in line 2 follows the same principle. **createFolder()** is a method and they have to be written in camel case otherwise they won't work, whereas functions and variables don't have to be but it's common practice to do it.

Note, that **DriveApp** isn't written in camel case. This is because **DriveApp** is a class and like methods, has to be written in a certain way. In this case, we start with a capital letter and put one on the A for App.

Arrays
Above we have seen that we can store values in a variable. Well, we can also store multiple values. To do so in an organized way, we can use an array.

In the example below, we have a set of 3 numbers which are stored in the variable called *numberArray*.

I'm going to log the contents of *numberArray* and also I'm going to get the first number in that array. To do that, we get the variable and then follow it with its position in square brackets.

Note, that array positions start at 0, so the first position is position 0, the second position 1, and so on.

```
function example5() {
  var numberArray = [45, 23, 10];
  Logger.log(numberArray);
  Logger.log(numberArray[0]);
}
```

As you can see below, it's logged the contents of the array. Note in the log, arrays are represented by square brackets.
In the second line, it's extracted the first number, which was in position 0. Note, this is now just a normal value and not an array anymore.

Info	[45.0, 23.0, 10.0]
Info	45.0

Further Reading

Here are some places I recommend you check out to learn even more about Apps Script.

I have the following books on Apps Script, which get progressively more complex:

Other Apps Script books by this author available on Amazon:

Beginner's Guide to Google Apps Script 1 – Sheets	<ul><li>This book goes through the basics of JavaScript and Apps Script.</li><li>It then goes through the SpreadsheetApp and the main classes: Spreadsheet, Sheet, and Range</li><li>Filled with dozens of examples of how to use Apps Script with Google Sheets.</li></ul>
Beginner's Guide to Google Apps Script 2 – Forms	<ul><li>This book goes through using Apps Script with **Google Forms**.</li><li>It covers:<ul><li>Creating and updating Google Forms</li><li>Adding different types of questions to a form</li><li>Using form responses</li><li>Adding form validation</li></ul></li></ul>

	- Adding page navigation – making a clocking in & out form - Making quizzes in Forms
Step-by-step Guide to Google Apps Script 4 – Documents	- This book goes through using Apps Script with **Google Docs** - It covers: - Creating a Google Doc from a form submission - Master Document copier - Edit a document template using placeholders - Making an invoice with multiple items - Making a document from scratch - Making student reports with progress bars - Emailing reports as a PDF or as a link - Creating multiple reports in one document - Emailing specific conference information - Sending conference info via a web app - Update document from data on the web

Google Apps Script Projects 1	• This book goes through 8 real-world practical projects step-by-step to help you practise your Apps Script skills. • Projects: -Book inventory -Make sheets and documents per student -Placement test -Copy folder content -Set up new employee -Issues reporting with translation -Multiple files and folder maker -Send certificates to students
Google Apps Script Projects 2	• This book goes through 8 real-world practical projects step-by-step to help you practise your Apps Script skills. Projects: • Mail merge using draft emails • Make multiple short URL links for pre-filled Google Forms • Date maker taking holidays into account • Send emails: 6 easy-to-use templates • Creating Calendar events and Meet links • Online exam maker • Extracting data from Excel

	• Book Inventory: Web app
JavaScript Fundamentals for Apps Script Users	• This book explains all the fundamental concepts in JavaScript. To use Apps Script well, it's important to have a solid understanding of JavaScript. • It will take you through areas such as, variables, data types, functions, string methods, template literals, dates, conditionals, arrays, array methods, array iteration, loops, and objects. All with useable examples in Apps Script. It also comes with files which contain all the examples.

All available on Amazon as paperback books and ebooks.

Apps Script Websites

https://developers.google.com/apps-script/reference

This is Google's official Apps Script site, which contains lists of Apps Script code that you'll need for your programs. In a lot of cases, it'll give you example chunks which you can copy and paste right into your program. Bookmark it, you'll be using it a lot!

GOOGLE APPS SCRIPT GOOGLE GROUP COMMUNITY
This community is full of wonderful people willing to share ideas and to help you if you get stuck. It's growing all the time and just shows how popular Apps Script is becoming.

https://groups.google.com/forum/#!forum/google-apps-script-community

FEEDBACK
I would love to hear your thoughts on this book! It would be great, if you could spare a minute to fill in this short feedback form:
bit.ly/BazsBooks
Thank you!
Barrie "Baz" Roberts

WWW.BAZROBERTS.COM
You will find further ideas on how to use Apps Script and Google Workspace on my website:
www.bazroberts.com

Other books and ebooks available by this author on Amazon:

Beginner's Guide to Google Drive	Beginner's Guide to Google Sheets	Beginner's Guide to Google Docs	Google Sheet Functions – A step-by-step guide
Step-by-step guide to Google Forms	Step-by-step guide to Google Sites	Step-by-step guide to Google Slides	Step-by-step guide to Google Meet

Rev 6

Printed in Great Britain
by Amazon